30-Days for Success

The Simple Solution to Master Your Thinking & Life

James M Murphy

Evolution For Success

ISBN: 1497467144
ISBN-13: 9781497467149

DEDICATION

To my beautiful wife, Emma. I will never be married to you long enough. Nicolas and Isabelle; you are miracles, our gifts from God. I am thankful for all of you, everyday.

A very special Thank You to one of the best coaches on the planet, Debbie DeVoe. You are an amazing editor and friend. It's been a great ride from our early years coaching with Tony Robbins, to Money Mastery in Aspen, to a great summer in Larkspur and beyond!

To all of my clients, many of whom I now count as my dearest friends, I wouldn't be here without you! Thank you!

"Progress is impossible without change, and those who cannot change their minds, cannot change anything."   ~ George Bernard Shaw

"Tempest-tossed souls, wherever ye may be, under whatsoever conditions ye may live, know this--in the ocean of life the isles of Blessedness are smiling, and the sunny shore of your ideal awaits your coming. Keep you hand firmly upon the helm of thought. In the barque of your soul reclines the commanding Master; he does not sleep; wake him. Self-control is strength; Right Thought is mastery; Calmness is power. Say unto your heart, "Peace. Be Still."" ~ James Allen, "As a Man Thinketh"

CONTENTS

DAY

HOW TO USE THIS BOOK

Welcome to 30-Days for Success. This book will allow you to change your life
through mastery of...

the Simple Solution.

This is a special, unique 30-Day program that is designed for one thing...

To change your thinking, which will change your feelings, which will change your actions, which will change your Life's Results!

I imagine most people like to start with a goal setting program but not here. Think about it, a person can't make a great goal in a bad state. They can only make a great goal in a great state. But what makes a great state? Having a mental, emotional, physical and spiritual state that is all in alignment.

Have you heard the famous story told by Dr. Russell Conwell? In his famous speech, "Acres of Diamonds" he tells the story of Al Hafed, who lived on the banks of the River Indus in modern day Baghdad.

He was a content wealthy man because he owned a nice little farm with orchards and gardens. Al Hafed had some extra cash and a beautiful family, so he was very comfortable and content. One night, an old priest visited him and told him the story of how the worlds earth was made, which included telling about the formation of rocks, precious metals and stones.

Al Hafed was amazed to hear about the riches of the earth and the value of precious stones. He decided he had to have a diamond mine so he could grow many more farms. The poison of discontent slowly started to permeate his thoughts.

Eventually, he sold everything he owned and went in search of diamonds, across Persia, Palestine and into Europe. A few years later, with his money, family and orchard gone, he found himself alone, despondent and dismayed. As he was walking along the beach, a large wave swept in from the sea and took him away.

Meanwhile, back on the farm, the man who had purchased Al Hafed's land had something interesting happen. One day, as he was tending to the orchard and watering his animals from the stream on the property, there was glint of light in the watery sand. With interest, he reached down, discovered a shiny rock, took it home and placed it on the mantle piece.

A few weeks later the same priest came through, and while staying the night; noticed it. Picking it up he exclaimed, "it's a diamond!" What the new owner found, was the first diamond to be pulled from one of the richest diamond mines in history; the mines of Golconda which went on to literally yield, "acres of diamonds."

This book will give you **The Simple Solution** to access the riches of your life. ***Your diamond mine lies within your mind.*** As you progress along this program and your thinking shifts, several things will occur.

First, what you are already doing in your life will change. You will see results in your daily life by seemingly small coincidences happening and as you progress, these moments will grow.

Second, you will experience thoughts and moments of possibility. You may find yourself saying, "wow, maybe I can do this" and then will begin to notice even more coincidences occurring to make it happen.

Third, when doing correctly, over time all complaining and dissatisfaction will disappear from your reality. This is when you know the book is really starting to work.

There will be a lot of repetition in this book. That is on purpose to anchor into your mind consciously and unconsciously the thought patterns necessary for success. Mastery comes through repetition over and over and over and over and over again! Be diligent and read everyday like it was the first time!

Fourth, there will be days your "conditioned mind" will tell you to not do the exercises. Like any growth, pushing through resistance is important. Sometimes you will have to push yourself to do these exercises. Be purposeful in working to master **The Simple Solution**. Discipline yields results.

Finally, do each days morning and evening exercises in order. If you miss one, no problem. No matter what the exercises are, always default back to mastering **The Simple Solution**.

Perfection stinks...forgive yourself for missing a day, pick up right where you are and push forward! As they say, "Anything worth doing...is worth doing badly the first few times."

You will have to do daily writing to complete this journey so find something nice to work with to keep organized. This book is designed for you to take notes in or you can get a good journal so you can write to your hearts content. I would also suggest getting a nice pen that you feel good with, along with a pack of note cards.

You can get additional support on the 30-Days for Success Facebook Page. Friend us!

Once you have these items in hand...let's get started!

"The secret to change is to focus all of your energy, not on fighting the old, but on building the new."   ~ Socrates

My 30-Day Promise

Today is the first day of the rest of my life. I fully commit and promise to persevere in completing this book in its entirety, starting today.

_____/_____/_____

I understand that in order to achieve all that I desire in this life, success lies at managing the risk found at the end of my comfort zone. I strive for excellence and realize that the real work in life begins right at the moment everyone else says they have done enough, quits and goes home. I will stay focused and committed to this book even when they entice me to go with them.

I promise to keep in the front of my mind at all times, **The Simple Solution** and strive to achieve mastery of this one simple principle. I will celebrate my wins and honor my failures, knowing that working through both will lead me to a new life of Success.

I will stand guard at the doorway of my mind and promise to feed it only positive messages mentally, emotionally, physically and spiritually. I will focus on achievement of my goals one day at a time and stay away from looking back over my shoulder to the past or dreaming too far forward into my future. That is where distraction and doubt lie in wait to ambush my success.

To all of this I promise for the next 30 Days, I will put in the time needed to complete this book, Honor my word and respect myself.

I am worthy of the success that I desire!

Signature _____

DAY #1
THE SIMPLE SOLUTION

MORNING: Good Morning! Today is going to be simple. Grab a cup of water, coffee or juice and let's get down to business.

Now...in this moment...NOW...is power. In your thinking, feeling, seeing, and believing in a better future for yourself...the only power you will ever have to create your new life, new habit or new thinking pattern, is in this very moment...NOW.

You might say, "but what about the past? All of this, and that, happened to me and it's made me who I am." There is no denying that your past has created the results you have now. As a matter of fact, who and what you are now is the sum total of all of the conscious *and unconscious* decisions you have made in your life up to this point. That can all change when you choose it to let it go and think differently.

Everything is energy and all energy or movement in nature has a cause and effect. There is always a natural consequence, most especially with our thoughts.

That said, if you want something different in your life now, you have to think differently now. You have to be willing to release the need to think the thoughts based on your past, so that you can make space for thoughts and beliefs that will create different results in your future.

I promised to reveal **The Simple Solution** that will change your life. It is so powerful in its simplicity that you may believe it's too good to be true, it can't be that simple. You may even want to throw it away.

Well, people throw pennies away every day too, The U.S. Mint makes about 13 billion pennies a year and half of these pennies will disappear from circulation within a year.

How much wealth is lost by discarding something that seems to small to make a difference? Every single thought has value and when they are accumulated over the course of a day, week, month and year; they accumulate to produce true wealth and change. So here it is...MASTER IT WELL!!!

The Simple Solution: With every thought, idea, decision, feeling or belief, *"SAY IT THE WAY YOU WANT IT TO BE!"*

Yes, it is just that simple! The brain does not register the word 'not.' Think about how often you hear people say, "I don't want to lose my job, I don't want to feel angry."

If I said, "**Don't** picture an <u>**orange striped skunk**</u> in your mind, right now," what did you see in your mind? Chances are it was the picture of an orange striped skunk. Try it again, don't see a blue pig.

Today's Exercise:

☐ Take out your first Notecard and write on it, "I promise and am committed to practice *saying it the way I want it to be!"*

☐ Write down everything that you *don't* want to happen today. Rewrite them, *"saying it the way I want it to be!"*

Here are some examples:

I hope I'm not late for work ~ I will arrive in a timely manner and all will be OK.

I hope traffic isn't bad ~ Traffic will flow as smooth as possible and I will be patient and calm.

I don't think I am going to be able to do this ~ I am going to find a creative solution to every problem that comes my way.

<u>What you *don't* want</u>	<u>The way you want it to be</u>

☐ For the rest of the day, focus and practice, ***"saying it the way you want it to be!"*** Stop and rephrase your thoughts and speech every time you hear or think something in the negative.

I know what you are thinking, "RIGHT...like that is going to make a difference." Well, remember that 13 billion pennies a year is a little more than 1.08 billion pennies a month. If you collected the half of those that were lost, that would be about 504 million pennies, which would be about 5.04 million dollars. You can and will become rich as you start to change your thoughts!

☐ Place reminders in your car, bathroom mirror, bedroom, computer, time management system, iCloud, Outlook, anywhere you can, and ***"say it the way you want it to be!"***

☐ In addition, notice how often you and others, use the word 'not' in their speech. Rephrase every sentence you use into the positive, and ***"say it the way you want it to be!"***

I will see you later tonight for the evening exercise.

NOTES:

EVENING #1

Good Evening, how was your day? Did you practice, *"saying it the way you wanted it to be?"* How often did you use and/or hear other people use the word 'not' in their language and get exactly what they didn't want?

I hope that the exercise was more difficult than you thought because that means that you really worked at creating a better neurological connection throughout the day. This evenings exercise is simple.

☐ Now that you have started to practice, *"saying it the way you want it to be!"* in your life, jot down some thoughts about the way you want your day to be tomorrow. As you write them, *"the way you want it to be,"* also speak them **OUT LOUD.**

_____

_____

_____

_____

_____

_____

_____

_____

Picture yourself having them one by one as you fall asleep in bed. What you focus on 20-30 minutes before bed is what your unconscious mind focuses on all night while you sleep. Reviewing your outcomes right before bed ensures your unconscious mind will be putting its full power to finding the resources to make them become a reality.

See you tomorrow for Day #2.

DAY #2
TIME TO HAVE A PARTY!

MORNING: Let's start with a quick recap of yesterday! Grab your journal, note cards and your morning cup of something and let's get down to business.

The only moment of true power lies in this moment...NOW. The ability to think, feel, and see a better future for yourself starts NOW. The human brain does not process the word, 'not.' What you don't want is exactly what you will receive. The power to change lies in your MIND first, not the external world. There are acres of diamonds waiting to be discovered there!

This entire book revolves around providing tools for your MASTERY of **the SIMPLE SOLUTION**: ***"say, think, feel and see your life the way you want it to be!"***

Thoreau once said, "If you have built castles in the sky, let not your dreams go to waste; just build the foundations under them."

"Saying it the way you want it to be!" will help you to build the foundations under your castle.

As you start to change your thinking and speaking, there will be an interesting natural consequence. If you are ***"saying it the way you want your life to be!"*** you will naturally STOP thinking and speaking about your problems, stresses, challenges, aches and pains or mental patterns of scarcity and fear.

STOP and reread this last paragraph until you really understand what I am saying!

When someone says how are you feeling today, you will have to respond, "I find myself getting better and better every moment."

"How's business today?" becomes "I'm finding new ways to overcome my challenges and I'm finding new solutions to generate cash flow."

Or, "How was that job evaluation today?" turns into "It was a great meeting where I found what I am doing great and how I can improve to get that next raise."

Now, you can expect to hit some resistance as you work to change your thinking. THAT'S THE POINT! You are creating new thought patterns and neurological connections. You have to FAKE IT UNTIL YOU MAKE IT! Persistence is KING!

Today's Exercise:

☐ Keep your first note card and review it regularly throughout the day.

☐ Create a second note card, _**"I choose to say, think, feel and see my life the way I want it to be!"**_ Review it regularly throughout the day and repeat **OUT LOUD**.

☐ Get others to join in the 'not' Game. Find 3-5 people, (kids are great at this game) get them to help you to _**"say it the way you want it to be!"**_ ALL OF THE TIME.

☐ Find a way to make this be Fun! For example, set up a game where every time either you and/or one of them isn't _**"saying it the way you/they want it to be!"**_, there is a consequence. It could be 25 cents in a 'not' jar, whoever keeps the lowest score each day wins, you decide your consequences and KEEP IT FUN!

REMEMBER, the easiest way to check your progress is to keep alert for responses that are negative or where you are telling people about your problems. That's not, _**"saying it the way you want it to be!"**_ (did you catch how I used 'not' in that sentence? Just a clue for tomorrow's fun!)

I will see you later tonight for the evening exercise.

NOTES:

EVENING: #2

Good Evening. Well, how was your day? Are you getting better at *"saying it the way you want it to be?"*

I hope that you raised your level of commitment today and followed through with the exercises. If you don't have even a minimal level of resistance to them each day, you are not working this program to its fullest. When you overcome that resistance, you are changing your life and moving more towards who you want to become.

☐ Write down your successes from today, *"saying it the way you want it to be!"* MAKE SURE you stay away from that perfectionist, "how could I have done it better junk! Only focus on your successes.

_____

_____

_____

_____

☐ Add: *"How do I see, think and feel my day tomorrow, the way I want it to be?"*

_____

_____

_____

_____

A person could fall asleep soundly tonight knowing they are going to continue to be moving towards *"who and what they want to be"* in their life. Sweet dreams and see you tomorrow for Day #3.

DAY #3
STOP BEING SO NEGATIVE

Are you excited? I AM! WHY? Take a moment and in your mind, walk through your day. Did you *"see it the way you want it to be!"* or did you see it the way you did 'not' want it to be?

Today is going to be fun because we are going to talk about one of my favorite language patterns that may also be keeping you from the success that you deserve.

So, let's continue on our journey of mastering *"saying it the way you want it to be!"*

Building the foundation of your dreams takes planning and purpose. Any mason knows that the most important part of building any structure is the proper placement and setting of the "cornerstone." Historically, the cornerstone of any building is critical because all of the other stones will be set in reference to it. It alone determines how the rest of the building will be arranged.

<u>Our Cornerstone</u> is "SAYING IT THE WAY YOU WANT IT TO BE!"

Sometimes our mind resists suggestions and new beliefs, why? Just because it can, it enjoys taking the path of least resistance.

We've discussed the language pattern of the word 'NOT.' Remember the human brain does not register the word 'not.'

Let's take a look at another language pattern that could be robbing you from your life being, *"the way you want it to be!"* The thief is the word, **'but.'**

Beware of working to *"say it the way you want it to be!"* and then linking that statement to another statement with the word 'but.'

Here's a scenario:

<u>Child:</u> "What was my grade on the test?"

<u>Teacher:</u> "You did really awesome getting an 'A' on the test ***but*** you got two problems wrong."☐☐

Write down what you remember from that last statement. _____

Was your first impression that the child got two problems wrong?

18

⬚Taking words like, "but, although, however, still, even though...." out of your speech will magnify your results when you are, *"saying it the way you want it to be!"*

If needed, substitute 'but' with the word 'AND.' In the previous scenario it would have been better for the teacher to respond with, "You did really awesome getting an 'A' on the test *and* you got 96% of the problems right." What would the child remember then?

Today's Exercise:

☐ Continue to *"say it the way you want your life to be!"*

☐ Practice removing words like, "but, although, however..." from your speech. Remember, they negate the positive aspects of *"saying it the way you want it to be!"*

☐ Replace **'but'** with the word **'AND'** every chance you get. Literally, stop in mid-sentence and rephrase your thought from the beginning, loudly enunciating the word **'AND.'**

☐ Write one thing you want to happen today, *"saying it the way you want it to be!"*

_____

Continue to build a solid foundation in your mind how you want your life to be. Build that muscle!

EVENING #3

Well, how was your day today? Did taking 'but' out of your vocabulary and replacing it with the word 'and' work? I bet it took some mental effort to *"saying it the way you wanted it to be!"*

☐ After 3 days of, *"saying it the way you want it to be!"* in your life, how have things changed?

Have you noticed that you're talking about your problems less? Are people responding to you differently? Have you seen or experienced any coincidences happening from the changes you've made in the way that you are speaking?

_____

_____

_____

When your thinking shifts, so does your external world. As you clear up the clutter inside, the outside must also change.

☐ Rewrite what you want in the next 30-Days, *"the way you want it to be"* and repeat them **OUT LOUD**. Continue to picture yourself having them one by one as you fall asleep in bed.

_____

_____

_____

_____

_____

See you tomorrow for Day #4 where we will dig another level deeper into creating change within. We will explore how to create deep and lasting change in regards to your identity.

DAY #4
'I AM' THE POWER OF IDENTITY

Good Morning and let me start the day off by saying, "You are AWESOME for making it to Day #4."

If you are starting to waver in your motivation or challenged with the program, that means you are right on track. Let me explain why.

Do you remember what I stated in the beginning what the outcome of this book was? "To change your thinking."

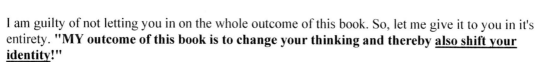

Well, I imagine that by Day #4, the anticipation, excitement, and expectation of learning and changing your life is starting to wear off. It may be getting OLD to hear one more time, **COME ON...YOU CAN DO IT!!!** *"think, feel and say it the way you want it to be!"*

I am guilty of not letting you in on the whole outcome of this book. So, let me give it to you in it's entirety. **"MY outcome of this book is to change your thinking and thereby <u>also shift your identity</u>!"**

Change in life is a marathon race, not a sprint! People tend to want it ALL now and if they can't have it all right now, then most just quit! Hence the saying, "success starts the minute everyone else quits."

When people learn that I ran a 100-mile Ultra-marathon in just over 24 hours, sometimes I get the response, "I could never do that, I'm not a runner." This always makes me smile because walking and running are *exactly the same body movement*. You just keep your head up and put one foot 12 inches in front of the other.

So physiologically, saying you are not a runner is like saying you can't walk. What makes the difference? **Their identity!** Who they perceive themselves to be is the key.

Look at the picture above of my American Curl cat named Chip! We were watching a show with my daughter about lions in Africa. He stayed that way for 30 minutes, glued to the TV. It seemed obvious that at a deep level, in his core, he relates and feels like a lion even though on the outside he is a cat!

Everyone acts in accordance with their CORE IDENTITY; who they *perceive* themselves to be. IDENTITY work is some of the deepest, most fundamental change a person can make within themselves. However, many people never really stop and connect with who they really are inside.

21

If the changes you are looking to make seem to be going slower it could be because you are challenging your personal identity. I'm sure you have experienced a moment of, **"saying it the way you want it to be"** and hearing yourself respond with, "yeah, right, I don't believe that for a second." In those moments your identity is resisting taking on the new beliefs because they are not congruent with your current beliefs or identity.

Today, we are working to create new identity statements in our pursuit of mastering **"thinking, feeling and saying it the way you want it to be!"** In order to write out some core identity statements that will carry deep meaning for you, take out your journal and answer the following:

1. Find 3-5 traits or behaviors that you exhibit and don't like. Example: "I am a procrastinator and don't want to wait until the last minute to write my social media articles."

2. For each statement, answer the following. "What benefit do I get from this negative behavior?" (answering this will take some effort-the core of most procrastination is fear of rejection and/or not trusting that something will happen!) Example: "I feel like I have to be perfect, so if I procrastinate and do it last minute then I can just turn it in as good enough and not have to get any feedback from others, which I take as rejection and not being good enough."

3. Create a NEW core identity statement that is the opposite of the benefit of the negative behavior. Example: "I, James Murphy, produce great quality work and <u>feel safe, comfortable and confident in sharing</u> my thoughts and ideas with others. I easily <u>accept</u> feedback as other's opinions and ideas knowing that some points will be valid and others I can pass on.

Notice how the underlined parts are the opposite of the fear based piece.

Today's Exercise:

☐ Write 5 new statements, **"thinking, feeling and saying it the WAY YOU WANT TO BE!"** The new statements should support your new ways of, **"thinking, feeling and saying it the way you want it to be!"** You will know when you have this correctly because the little, "yeah, right" voice, will stop!

<u>Here are some examples:</u>

"My name is James Murphy and today I see, hear, think and know that I am courageous in pursuing my business challenges, fearless when it comes to managing risk and focused on my long term goals."

"I, James Murphy, see, hear, feel think and know that in every fiber of my being, I approach the world with focused determination *"saying it the way I want it to be!"* This creates a world of possibility for me, my family and the achievement of my goals."

"I, James Murphy, stay connected to my truth today and stand firm in my convictions while remaining a humble servant empowering others."

Write these on your note cards and repeat throughout the day!

☐ Second, continue to create awareness in your thoughts and speech as well as other peoples. Continue to practice, *"saying it the way you want your life to be!"*

NOTES:

"I, _____, see, hear, feel think and know that I AM

_____.

EVENING #4

Hello and Good Evening,

Well, how was your day? Did you practice, ***"saying it the way you wanted it to be!"*** in regards to your new identity? Repetition can be boring sometimes but remember that mastery comes from repeating an experience so often that you finally do it subconsciously. Tomorrow we will explore the pattern of learning.

This evenings exercise is simple.

☐ In order to anchor in the identity statements, pick your favorite one and rewrite it separately 5 times while you ***"say it the way you want it to be!"*** **OUT LOUD.**

_____

_____

_____

_____

_____

_____

_____

_____

Picture yourself being each one as you fall asleep in bed.

See you tomorrow for Day #5.

DAY #5
THE LEARNING LADDER

Good Morning Sunshine! That is how I wake up my daughter everyday!

Today is going to be a great day as we continue to master **The Simple Solution**, *"seeing, hearing and thinking my life, the way I want it to be!"*

Now...in this moment...NOW...is power and repetition is the mother of all skill. When I started to learn hypnosis and the different language patterns, I would print on a notecard, one language pattern, put it on my computer keyboard and use it in every coaching call I had that day. By the end of the month, I had mastered the language patterns into my speech so they were easy and effortless.

There are 4 steps to the learning ladder that everyone goes through to master a skill. The first rung of the ladder: Unconsciously Incompetent (UI). Before you started reading this book you were Unconsciously Incompetent. You just didn't know, that you didn't know, about **The Simple Solution**. It wasn't in your awareness.

Now that you've begun reading this book, something changes because now you've been exposed to **The Simple Solution**. You had a moment of awareness and moved up the ladder and became Conscious of your Incompetence (CI). You became aware of something you weren't aware of before. Awareness is a powerful tool because it opens up choices in life.

Once you became aware and were able to see choices in your life, you decided to take different actions, like get a journal, note cards, and do the daily exercises. This allows you to step up to the third rung; building Conscious Competence (CC).

However, there is a stumbling block between these two steps. In order to get to the last rung of the ladder we continue for a while to cycle between Conscious Incompetence (CI) and Conscious Competence (CC). During this revolving cycle we struggle to develop the new habits and behaviors.

This is the work stage in the learning ladder. You have to consciously choose to take actions, sometimes succeeding. We rotate between sometimes failing and being Consciously Incompetent then taking new actions and trying again to reach being Consciously Competent.

As this cycle continues, the work becomes easier and the results become greater. As you repeat this cycle over and over to master the skill, you will eventually move to the highest rung of the learning ladder. You become Unconsciously Competent (UC). Here, you can finally perform the task without thinking about it because of the hard work you put in to master the middle two steps. It has become a new unconscious habit.

One thing to remember! It is impossible for any person to jump from being Unconsciously Incompetent to Unconsciously Competent.

Andre Agassi, used to hit 2,500 tennis balls a day at 7 years old! He would never have been able to go from, "here's a racket" to "grand slam" winner without the practice and mastery of the Learning Ladder.

Take heart in the exercises today and practice hitting the ball. Go back to your singular note card and practice, *"seeing, hearing, thinking and feeling everything in your life just the way you want it to be!"* Keep hitting those thoughts inside your mind, just like Agassi hit those tennis balls, quicker, faster and harder. Think them *"the way that you want them to be!"*

The Simple Solution: With every thought, idea, decision, feeling or belief, *"SAY IT THE WAY YOU WANT IT TO BE!"*

Today's Exercise:

☐ Continue to practice, *"seeing, hearing, thinking and feeling everything in your life the way you want it to be!"* Stop and rephrase any thought you speak, hear or think in the negative.

☐ **RE-DO** all of the reminders in your car, bathroom mirror, bedroom, computer, time management system, iCloud, Outlook. Shift them around so that you will see them differently.

I will see you later tonight for the evening exercise.

NOTES:

EVENING #5

Good Evening,

Well, how was your day? Did you practice, *"saying it the way you wanted it to be?"*

This evenings exercise is simple.

☐ Write out a detailed explanation of exactly how you want tomorrow to be. If you typically experience low or no energy during the day or are concerned about a potential meeting, rewrite those moments, *"saying it the way you want it to be!"* **OUT LOUD.**

_____

_____

_____

_____

_____

_____

☐ Talk yourself through your day tomorrow, *"the way you want it to be!"*

Having a tough time visualizing? Stay tuned for Day #6 because I am going to teach you the most foolproof way to visualize. I assure you, it's never been written about this way in any other self-help materials I have read over the past 15 years!! You will experience success with it...I Promise!

See you tomorrow for Day #6.

DAY #6
SEE YOUR SUCCESS

Good Morning! It is going to be a Fantastic Day!

Remember **The Simple Solution:** with every thought, idea, decision, feeling or belief, ***"SAY IT THE WAY YOU WANT IT TO BE!"***

Today we are going to focus on adding a very specific tool into the process ***"saying it the way you want it to be,"*** it's called *visualization*.

You have probably heard examples of how successful people like Tiger Woods, "see" the shot before taking it. Before he hits the ball, he pictures himself making the shot and in his mind, "sees" the golf ball going into the hole. Visualization is critical to success because it programs the mind to "see" specifically what you want it to build, create or produce. It is important to know where you are going.

One of the challenges of visualization is that people do not consciously understand how the process works inside the mind. At least, that was until today. This the most foolproof way to visualize.

In the science of Neuro Linguistic Programming, (NLP), it was discovered there are threee main ways people process their experiences; Visual (seeing), Auditory (saying) or Kinesthetic (feeling). One way to discover how people code their experiences is through watching their eye movements. If a person looks up and to the right or left, they are visually "seeing" a picture in their mind that is being recalled/remembered or constructed/created.

In order to find whether up and to the right or up and to the left is your "visual remember," close your eyes and looking up and to your left, picture your bedroom as a child, your first car, or a picture of your mom or dad's face. Was it easy to "see?"

Now close your eyes and reverse the process looing looking up and to the right. Was it easier or harder to picture the color of your first car, your mom and dad's face or a picture of your pet?

Now, close your eyes and "see," a Green polka dot skunk looking up and to your right. Was it easy to see that green polka dot skunk there? Do it again looking up and to the left. Which was easier? Up and to your right? Or up and to your left?

Now that you have the hang of it, close your eyes and picture your first bicycle or favorite toy as a child. Was it easier for you to "see" it looking up and to the right or up and to the left?

28

You will have experienced one of the two following patterns.

1. It will be easier for you to look up and to your left to visually recall/remember and up and to your right to visually construct/create a picture.

   or

2. It will be easier for you to look up and to your right to visually recall/remember and up and to your left to visually construct/create a picture.

How is this helpful?

When we are using **The Simple Solution,** *"Seeing it the way we want it to be!"* If you are saying something like, "I don't want to lose my keys again," you are creating that picture in your mind. When you reframe that same statement to *"seeing it to the way you want it to be,"* with "my keys are safe and I will remember exactly where I put them" it helps to create a new picture in your mind that matches. With your eyes closed, look up to the right or left to your visual construct/create and "SEE" yourself putting them exactly in that right place where you will remember seeing them safe. Imagine remembering where you put them next time you need them.

Today's Exercise:

☐ **First step:** Write down something that you would like to "See" yourself Being, Doing or Having. Keep it simple; maybe a new computer, toaster or coffee press.

Example: I want have a new white toaster.

_____

☐ **Second step:** write out the answer to this question, what is the very last thing that needs to happen in order for you to be convinced that you have achieved that want/goal?

Example: I imagine my kitchen counter with a brand new white toaster with two toaster slots, chrome top, white cord and lever.

_____

☐ **Third step:** Stop and meditate on the picture inside your mind. Close your eyes and look up to the right or left. Make the picture big and bright, with as many details as you can. Take two minutes in the morning and at night to visualize your goal with your eyes closed.

At first, you will probably only be able to hold your focus on the picture for 5-10 seconds. When the picture goes away, just open your eyes for a couple seconds, then close them and look up to the left or right again and "see" the picture and make it big and bright again. Repeat as necessary. You will find that eventually you will be able to hold the picture for up to 60 seconds or more.

I will see you later tonight for the evening exercise.

NOTES:

EVENING #6

Good Evening. Well, how was your day? Did you practice, *"Seeing it the way you wanted it to be?"*

For your visualization exercise tonight:

☐ Rewrite your goal from this morning.

☐ Rewrite the very last thing that has to happen in order for you to know you have achieved that goal.

☐ Close your eyes, look to your visual construct/create, *"seeing it the way you want it to be!"*

☐ ADD one more piece to your visualization. To get motivated to achieve it, as you picture it up and to your right or left, slide the picture so that it is right down in front of your face. With as much detail as possible, when it feels good, hold it for as long as you can.

☐ Repcat as you fall asleep!

See you tomorrow for Day #7.

DAY #7
VISUALIZATION CONTINUED

Good Morning,

I sincerely hope that you are going to continue to have an amazing day today! Today is an additional practice day for mastering the art of visualization.

Let's review the visualization process.

The Simple Solution: You are going to practice, ***"SEEING IT THE WAY YOU WANT IT TO BE!"***

Today's Exercise:

☐ Write down a goal that you want to have, ***"the way that you want it to be!"***

_____

☐ What is the very last thing that needs to happen in order for you to know you have achieved it?

_____

☐ Recall if your visual construct/create is up and to your right or up and to your left.　　**R　　L**

☐ Close your eyes and looking up to your visual construct/create, picture that very last thing.

Picture it with as much detail as your can and slide it right down in front of your face. Hold the image for as long as you can, anywhere from 5-60 seconds. Repeat.

☐ **BONUS:** As you get better and better at the visualization process, keep adjusting the picture until it feels the best. With your eyes closed, repeat the following steps. When the picture is straight in front of you get curious and notice how your feelings to the picture change as you bring it closer and further away, change the color of the picture to black and white and then back to color, still to moving, framed or panoramic. Make sure you picture it looking through your own eyes and make sure you see yourself in the picture.

Play around with these 'sub-modalities' until you find where you "see" it feels the best. Repeat throughout the day.

An easy way to practice any new behavior is to link a habit with a habit. Do it while you are taking a shower, while going to the bathroom or before bed.

For today, just continue to practice, ***"seeing it the way you want it to be!"***

I will see you later tonight for the evening exercise.

NOTES:

EVENING #7

Good Evening,

Well, how was your day? Did you practice, ***"seeing it the way you want it to be?"***

I hope that the exercise has been getting easier and easier. The more you practice the easier it will become.

This evenings exercise is simple.

☐ Write down a goal that you want to have, ***"the way that you want it to be!"***

_____

☐ What is the very last thing that needs to happen in order for you to know you have achieved it?

_____

☐ Recall if your visual construct/create is up and to your right or up and to your left.   **R   L**

☐ Close your eyes and looking up to your visual construct/create, picture that very last thing that needs to happen in order to achieve it. Picture it with as much detail as your can and slide it right down in front of your face. Hold the image for as long as you can, anywhere from 5-60 seconds. Repeat.

"See your goals the way you want them to be!" Feel how good it feels to have completed them. Picture yourself having them one by one as you fall asleep in bed.

See you tomorrow for Day #8.

DAY #8
MASTERY OF MATERIALS

Good Morning! Today is about shifting information from your short term to long term memory. Grab a cup of water, coffee or tea and let's get down to business.

There is a simple concept in NLP that all high performance individuals know, "cells that fire together, wire together." What does this mean?

Learning to build new internal thoughts, beliefs and feelings is like building a road. At first, the road is just a deer path through the trees, then with time and human traffic, it becomes two rows of tire tracks.

As the path gets more traffic, gravel is put down. Then eventually it becomes an asphalt road. Then, with more traffic, it may turn into a 2-lane highway and over time cleared and made into an interstate or highway. It is easy for a country lane to go back to being overgrown but a 10-lane highway like the ones in California, it takes an earthquake to damage.

Our memory, performance and mastery of any thinking process or skill follows the same process.

Today we are going to widen the road so it can support more traffic. Review and read the concepts we have covered so far **OUT LOUD** to continue to pave the road to your success.

MASTERY:

The only place of power is right NOW!

What you have in your life now is the sum total of all of your conscious and unconscious thoughts and decisions you have made to date.

Space needs to be made for new thoughts and beliefs. Make that space by being willing to give up old thoughts and habits of thinking.

The mind does not register the word, 'not.'

Use it in a fun way to 'not' remember that using these skills can be fun and produce results easily and effortlessly.

Expand from not only saying it, but thinking, feeling and seeing your life *"the way you want it to be!"*

No one builds the foundations under their dreams alone. There will always be people to thank that have helped you along the way. It is only your pride that prevents you from asking for help. If you can't ask for and receive help, how can your graciously accept and receive what it is that you most want to have and create from the universe?

If you are practicing *"saying it the way you want it to be!"* you are probably noticing that you have drastically reduced talking to yourself and others about your problems and challenges.

Resistance happens because we have been working to change your beliefs by, *"saying it the way you want it to be!"* and at a deeper level those new beliefs may not match your deeper core identity.

People eventually have to change to adapt their actions to who they believe themselves to be in their core identity.

We all go through 4-Rungs of the Learning Ladder: UI-Unconsciously Incompetent, UC-Unconsciously Competent, CC-Consciously Competent & finally UC-Unconsciously Competent.

We can "see" things *"the way we want them to be!"*

People code their experiences with visual, auditory or kinesthetic cues.

Eye patterns are a pathway to recall and construct/create pictures, sounds and feelings in our mind.

Looking either up and to the right or left will either recall or construct/create pictures easily in our minds.

Visualizing pictures in our mind is easy once we discover our personal pattern.

Reinforce visualization by getting the picture you want to create and sliding it down right in front of your mind.

The Simple Solution: With every thought, idea, decision, feeling or belief, *"SAY IT THE WAY YOU WANT IT TO BE."*

Today's Exercise:

☐ Take any one of the concepts from the mastery review that you feel you are the weakest in, review the materials and redo the exercises from that day.

☐ Continue *"saying and seeing it the way you want it to be!"* Every time you hear or think something in the negative, STOP and rephrase it.

☐ Place *__NEW__* reminders in your car, bathroom mirror, bedroom, computer, time management system, iCloud, Outlook, anywhere you can and, *"see it the way you want it to be!"*

I will see you later tonight for the evening exercise.

NOTES:

EVENING #8

Good Evening,

Well, just over 1 week completed!

CONGRATULATE YOURSELF FOR COMING THIS FAR!

This evenings exercise is simple.

☐ **Without looking at your past notes; write down:**

- Everything that you have learned this past week.
- What have you discovered about your old thinking patterns?
- What have you experienced differently as a result of *"saying and seeing your life the way you want it to be?"*
- What have you learned about your core identity?
- Anything else that is important.

_____

_____

_____

_____

_____

_____

Tomorrow starts a new portion of the program. We are going to start to move into the structure of *how* to set goals even more purposefully and to *"live, say & see our lives the way we want them to be!"*

See you tomorrow for Day #9.

DAY #9
A PURPOSE DRIVEN LIFE

Good Morning! How about a 10-Minute power session on PURPOSE?

Everyone asks the question at one point and time, "What is the purpose of my life?" That is one BIG question to answer! After coaching and helping others to live purposeful lives for the last 15 years, (and having struggled to define my own), I have found the right question to discover what it is!

Purposeful people work everyday to "build and create a powerful emotional experience that is meaningful to them and empowers others to build and create their own powerful emotional experience."

Let's take an easy example, JK Rowlings built and created a powerful, emotionally charged experience for readers through her Harry Potter books. This emotional experience was meaningful to her because she obviously had a story that needed to be told deep inside, and, it empowered others to capture that emotional experience and spread it to different areas of their life! Parents read the books to their kids at night for emotional connection, people shared exciting moments at book releases with friends, and the talk of Harry Potter was an incredible emotional experience.

Take my mentor, Tony Robbins. He started by creating his weekend seminar experience, "Unleash the Power Within." With his painful childhood, it was certainly emotionally meaningful for him, and, who wouldn't be more empowered emotionally after walking across 12 feet of hot coals? People leave his seminars more emotionally charged with possibility for a better life than almost any other seminar ever created. They take that energy home and invest it into their businesses, relationships and 'building and creating' new things in their lives.

One last example; Look at every small business owner, entrepreneur, inventor, blog writer, real estate agent, financial planner, or anyone else. They are all looking for a better way to build and create something, a better way to express themselves so they can share those experiences with others.

Purpose 101. "What is the most true emotional expression of yourself, and what can you build or create with it, that when shared with others will move, motivate, inspire and empower them to find and share their own emotional expression of themselves?"

The key to answer that question lies in those moments from your past...I remember when I was in 7th grade walking home thinking I wanted to be a teacher. I liked school even though I never thought I was good at it. I liked to learn, share, and grow. I wanted to be a radio announcer in speech class when we did a radio show project. I made people laugh and they couldn't see me as the 'fat, shy kid.' I loved how music expressed emotion and helped me connect with myself. AND, I promptly talked myself out of doing any of those because they didn't 'make enough money.'

Fast forward to James Murphy at 45. I am an Executive Business Coach. I constantly read and educate myself, and share that knowledge through social media and coaching sessions (on the phone...almost like a radio announcer). I create podcasts, blog articles, teach and touch people with helping them create better emotional states in their minds and lives, and I LOVE public speaking. In essence, I am a teacher, just not in the context I had originally thought walking home from school that day.

You too, can start living a more purposeful life each day as you embrace the question, "what can I build and create that is an emotional expression of myself that will allow others to build and create more of what they want emotionally in life?" Then take inspired action to create it!

REMEMBER - **The Simple Solution:** With every thought, idea, decision, feeling or belief, *"SAY IT THE WAY YOU WANT IT TO BE!"*

Today's Exercise:

☐ Think back to when you were a child. What did you always want to be when you grew up? What were the powerful moments of your life when you said to yourself, "I really want to do that!" and then proceeded to talk yourself out of it?

_____

_____

_____

_____

_____

_____

_____

_____

☐ Write down all of the things that you love and are good at. If you had to do something for the rest of your life over and over again, what area of life would it be in? Or, if you had one day to live, and had to build and create something to leave as a legacy, what would you build or create? Or, what would you do over and over and over again because you loved it so much you would work through the boredom of the repetition of it? (ie, Tony has been doing the same UPW seminar for over 25 years and can you imagine how many times Lee Greenwood has sung, "Proud to be an American?")

_____

_____

_____

☐ "What can I build and create that is an emotional expression of myself, that will allow others to build and create more of what they want emotionally in life?"

_____

_____

_____

_____

☐ Today, see, hear, think &feel your purposeful life, *__the way you want it to be!__*

I will see you later tonight for the evening exercise.

EVENING #9

Good Evening,

Well, today was filled with some good brain work! How did the question of purpose work out?

I hope that the exercise was liberating and you discovered some good answers.

☐ **Continue to Journal:** "What can I build and create that is an emotional expression of myself, that will allow others to build and create more of what they want emotionally in life?"

_____

_____

_____

_____

_____

☐ Write out tomorrow, *"saying it the way you want it to be!"* and read it **OUT LOUD.** Visualize yourself moving through your day tomorrow as you fall asleep in bed.

_____

_____

_____

_____

See you tomorrow for Day #10.

DAY #10
MORE PURPOSE DRIVEN THOUGHTS

Today is a great day to build and create something wonderful with your life. Today is short and sweet, so grab your cup of coffee and let's get this train moving!

Remember that NOW…in this moment...NOW...is REAL Power. You now have in your hands, the two most POWERFUL TOOLS to change your life.

1. **The Purpose Question**: "What can I build and create with my unique skills and talents that will be emotionally meaningful for me and at the same time, inspire others emotionally and engage them to build and create their purposeful life that will motivate and inspire others?"

and…

2. What if everyone did #1 using **The Simple Solution**, *saying, thinking, feeling and seeing it the way they wanted it to be?*

Can you imagine a world where everyone was working on building and creating a unique expression of themselves that supported others to do the same?

There would be no problems in the world, everyone would be helping everyone, everyone would be confident in who they are, (not who they aren't), and there would be nothing but positive growth.

Purpose can be found in any action LARGE or small. A person creates a purposeful life by building and creating a thriving business practice that helps other to greater health JUST AS MUCH AS building and creating a more positive emotional experience by picking up a piece of trash in the parking lot (if you do it happily), share a smile with another person or go out of their way to help.

Remember, ABC. **A**lways **B**uild and **C**reate (that *purposeful, emotional expression* of you)

Today's Exercise:

☐ Come up with at least 10 ideas that you could build and create that would be meaningful and purposeful for you and for your life AND, as a result of you building them, would emotionally inspire others to do the same?

1. _____

2. _____

3. _____

4. _____

5. _____

6. _____

7. _____

8. _____

9. _____

10. _____

☐ All day today, stop, close your eyes, take a deep breath and ask yourself, "What can I build and create in this very moment?" As soon as an answer comes to you...DO IT! Practice, in your thinking, feeling, seeing, and believing in a better future for yourself, building and creating an emotional expression of you, even it if is the smallest act.

☐ **The Simple Solution:** Come up with a few ideas on what you can purposefully create in your life today with every thought, idea, decision, feeling or belief, ***"saying it the way you want it to be!"***

_____

_____

_____

_____

_____

_____

I will see you later tonight for the evening exercise.

NOTES:

EVENING #10

Good Evening,

I hope you were able to come up with at least 10 ideas for what you could build and create with your life. At this point, if you are frustrated with trying to figure our exactly what to build and create, remember, the purpose of the exercise is to shift your thinking to consistently ask and receive the answers to the question, "What can I build or create that is an emotional expression of myself?" Take any pressure off of yourself to, "find the right or final solution for your life."

Remember that we are building a road. It is better to keep travelling the dirt path and appreciate the dirt path instead of focusing on pushing it to become a super highway. Enjoy the process of discovering yourself. In due time all things will grow accordingly. Be comfortable asking the questions and be open to the answers.

☐ Continue to write down your thoughts on what you could build and create that would be an emotional expression of you.

_____

_____

☐ Continue to write down the *"way you want things to be!"* in your day tomorrow and read it **OUT LOUD** and visualize them as you go to bed.

_____

_____

See you tomorrow for Day #11.

DAY #11
ARE YOU TERRIFIED OF THE ANSWER?

Welcome to Day #11...we are officially over 1/3 of the way through your 30-Days for Success Program!! Congratulations!

Just one question for today, As you spent the last two days journaling and brainstorming the purpose question, "What could I build and create that would allow me to be emotionally fulfilled and by sharing it, would move, motivate and inspire others to do the same?" What answers did you come up with?

We chatted a few sessions ago about the moments that I had with being a teacher, using my voice to hear people laugh and loving learning. If you fast forward a bit in time, I remember the first day I was talking to a friend in California after I started working for Tony Robbins and telling him, "I want to take Tony's place when he is ready to stop his seminars. I want to be the next TR!" How far fetched was that? Very...BUT IT WAS MY DREAM! LIVING MY PURPOSE WAS WRAPPED UP IN THAT DREAM!

I will let you in on another secret: "IT TERRIFIED ME!"

What is on your list that's scary for you to contemplate, consider as a possibility or believe you could become? LIVING YOUR PURPOSE resides in those lofty thoughts and ideals! Just like when I was struggling to run 3 miles, a 100-mile race seemed impossible but there is purpose in higher goals.

Today's Exercise:

☐ Review your exercises for the last two days. Find the one idea that, "scares the heck out of you the most" and write it below.

_____

_____

_____

MOST PEOPLE FAIL BECAUSE THEY THINK TOO small, DREAM TOO small, LIVE TOO small, and as a result LOSE THEIR MOTIVATION and fall into the comfort zone of misery. That is a slow and painful death. A Purposeful person lives with courage and conviction and is always moving towards a LARGER future! There is purpose in pushing up against your comfort zone, growing, building, creating and working for something more .

People who are not purposeful...perish.

☐ If nothing on your list 'terrifies' you, then go back and brainstorm the question again until you come up with some ideas that do! (if all else fails, list something you have always wanted to do but never did, due to some limitations you put on yourself, i.e. go skydiving, take a martial arts class...).

_____

_____

☐ If you have more than one thing that terrifies the heck out of you, narrow the list down to the *one thing that terrifies you the most!*

_____

_____

☐ Imagine doing that thing that terrifies you the most. Write it down, ***"seeing, thinking and feeling it the way you want it to be!"***

_____

_____

☐ Write down the very last thing that would need to happen in order for you to know that you had achieved it."

_____

_____

_____

_____

_____

_____

NOTES:

EVENING #11

Good Evening,

Well, how was the excitement level in your life today? Did it increase as you thought about, pondered and contemplated that one thing that terrifies you the most? I hope you found that the more you focused on it, the less it terrified you and the more excited you became about it becoming real.

Repeat today's exercise to imprint the goal into your mind.

☐ Imagine doing that thing that terrifies you the most. Write it down, *"seeing, thinking and feeling it the way you want it to be!"*

_____

_____

_____

☐ Write down the very last thing that would need to happen in order for you to know that you had achieved it.

_____

_____

_____

As you fall asleep, visualize that very last thing that has to happen in order for you to achieve it.

*For you over-achievers, come up with a two or more things that terrify you the most and repeat!

See you tomorrow for Day #12, you're almost half way there!

DAY #12
WHAT DOES FEAR REALLY MEAN?

Good Morning! Let's hit it hard this morning, we have a serious topic to cover...FEAR!!!

Now...in this moment...NOW...is Power. The one thing that stops most people using that power to _LIVE_ an amazing, incredible and empowering life is...FEAR!

Fear is a powerful emotional state that is related to feeling scared, anxious, insecure, doubtful, panicked, alarmed, hesitant or mistrusting.

Fear prevents you from taking an action because of something you think may happen in the future that could harm you and/or create too much uncertainty in your future. Anxiety is related to fear in that it is a fear of the future. You have placed something in your mind for the future which is what you don't want to have happen. That is the opposite of **The Simple Solution** we are working to master.

So, what is needed to overcome fear? There are many positive emotional states to overcome fear. Some people rely on courage to take that first step. Some people rely on faith and trust, that everything will turn out OK in the end. The thing that is the lesson for today is the understanding that fear has a close cousin...excitement!

Yes, it's true, fear and excitement are two of the most closely linked physiological states there are. Imagine sitting in the front cart of a roller coaster. Out you shoot, up that first big hill...slowly up and up and up...then imagine being right at the top when there is a moment where time stops and you are suspended between going up and plunging headlong down the other side!

What is the difference between someone who throws up their hands, screams in delight and gets excited about the thrill of the ride and the person who clings onto the shoulder harness with a death grip, closes their eyes and prays for it to stop?

The answer is trust, faith, AND courage. Courage to try something new in the face of uncertainty, trust in being safe during the ride and faith that it will all turn out OK in the end. Faith, Trust and Courage come from, _**"seeing, thinking and feeling the end result the way you want it to be!"**_ NOT, from the fear driven pictures of, "seeing, thinking and feeling the end result the way you _don't_ want it to be."

That is the path and strategy to overcoming fear! _**"seeing, thinking and feeling the end result the way you want it to be,"**_ tips the scale from living in fear to living in excitement.

Remember **The Simple Solution:** With every thought, idea, decision, feeling or belief, *"SAY IT THE WAY YOU WANT IT TO BE!"*

Today's Exercise:

☐ Take your one thing that you answered from your PURPOSE question that terrified you the most.

Rewrite it until it creates a sense of excitement within you. Keep adjusting how you, *"see, hear and feel"* the very last thing that needs to happen in order for you to achieve it until you start to get excited.

☐ Answers these questions:

1. How can I have the courage to achieve this?

_____

_____

2. How can I trust that everything will be OK as I achieve this?

_____

_____

3. How can I engage my faith so I know this as a truth, that no matter what happens I will be OK?

_____

_____

_____

List these empowering beliefs, keep them in the positive, just *"the way you want them to be!"*

EVENING #12

Good Evening! Well, are you getting more comfortable with your purposeful goal? I hope so!

☐ Take your one thing that you answered from your PURPOSE question that terrified you the most. Rewrite it until it creates a sense of excitement within you.

☐ Answers these questions:

1. How can I have the courage to achieve this?

_____

_____

2. How can I trust that everything will be OK as I achieve this?

_____

_____

3. How can I engage my faith so I know this as a truth, that no matter what happens I will be OK?

_____

_____

_____

List these empowering beliefs, keep them in the positive, just *"the way you want them to be!"* Continue to re-write and review your exercise from this morning and visualize the end result as you go to sleep.

See you tomorrow for Day #13.

DAY #13
THE FUTURE

Good Morning! Today's 10-Minute routine is going to be fun. Grab a cup of water, coffee or juice and let's get EXCITED.

Write down your level of excitement for the day on a grading scale of A, B, C or D. _____

What grade did you give yourself?

If you are not at an A, but you are truly purposeful on building and creating something of value, what could be out of alignment? It could be your identity and how you see yourself.

Most people start the day focusing on what they need to DO in order to HAVE some results so then they can BE happy, successful, etc.

That order is backwards because if you are not happy and purposeful DO-ing, you may have the results but you will not BE-come who you want to be in the long term. Your identity and who you are BE-ing will not change. Eventually, you will fall back into your old habits and patterns.

You can see this pattern at the beginning of the New Year. People will start the gym, diet, lose weight and "do" drastic things. However, they never have their focus shift to 'Be-ing' happy and healthy, thinner and more energetic. How they see themselves is not the way they want it to be. Eventually, they go back to their original weight. Who they are BE-ing in their core identity never changed.

Shifting your thoughts to a more empowering identity is a great first step to creating a life that you desire. It must become a priority because it changes your identity and who you need to BE-come.

This may sound silly but when I was in college I was 240 lbs. There was this Dr. Pepper commercial where a guy used to jump around singing, "I'm a Pepper, you're a Pepper, wouldn't you like to be a Pepper too?" He was a young energetic guy, clean cut and all he had on was a pair of jeans and a plain white t-shirt. That image stuck in my mind and became my identity of how a healthy, energetic, fit guy should look. In my mind, I started to put my head on his body and that became my identity.

The more I focused on that picture in my mind, the more angry I got that I wasn't, and that pushed me to go out on a track at about midnight and run my first 3 miles. The more I pictured that guy with my face, the more I ran and eventually I 'BE-came' that guy.

Today's Exercise:

☐ Write down the way you want to "BE" today in an area of your life. Describe in detail how you want to 'BE' as a parent, spouse, employee, spiritual, physical, energetic and excited person.

_____

_____

_____

_____

_____

Today is Day #13, and for the next two days, I am going to push you hard to really create in your mind the identity of the person you want to BE. I want you to really ***"SEE, HEAR and FEEL yourself BEING the way you want yourself to BE!"***

See yourself now as that person who is purposefully building and creating every day, in every moment, balanced mentally, emotionally, physically and spiritually.

As we hit Day #16, you will have graduated from creating a new paradigm of thinking in both the short term and the long term with **The Simple Solution**: ***"SAYING, THINKING, SEEING AND FEELING IT THE WAY YOU WANT IT TO BE!"***

From there, we will be shifting to a more outward focus for the rest of the book in setting up some dynamic goals and focusing on the "DO-ing" and "Have-ing." First though, we have to focus on your new identity and "BE-ing."

I will see you later tonight for the evening exercise.

NOTES:

EVENING #13

Good Evening,

How was your level of excitement today "BE-ing" that purposeful person who was building and creating their life?

This evenings exercise is identity related again.

☐ Focus on rewriting your Identity of "BE-ing" purposeful. Write down how you *"say, hear, think, feel and see yourself being purposeful tomorrow."* Write down the description of what a purposeful day looks like, how you are focused, energized, "BE-ing" the person you want to be.

_____

_____

_____

_____

_____

_____

☐ Picture yourself going through tomorrow as that purposeful person, excited at building and creating as you fall asleep.

See you tomorrow for Day #14.

DAY #14
ANCHORING YOUR PURPOSEFUL IDENTITY

Good Morning! Grab your cup of coffee, tea, water and your journal.

Who are you today? What are you going to purposefully build and create?

How are you going to do it, ***"seeing, hearing, thinking and feeling it the way you want it to be?"***

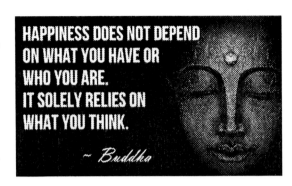

Now...in this moment...NOW...is Your Power. The time to change wasn't yesterday nor can it be tomorrow. The only time for change is right Now. The first way to change is to think differently about who you are.

I mentioned yesterday that I was going to push hard today to anchor in your new identity as a purposeful person who is building and creating a powerfully emotionally charged life and finding a way to share it with others.

Today we are going to put that identity to the test with a HUGE exercise!

ARE YOU READY?

Today's Exercise:

☐ Take out your journal and get your purposeful identity statement, who you are "BEING." Print it out on one of your note cards, BIG and legible. It should start with,

I,*(your name)*_____

am being _____

☐ Take your note card into your bathroom (you'll need a mirror), or in a private place, along with this book and your journal.

☐ Next, memorize your Identity and in front of the mirror, look deep into your eyes. Repeat your identity to yourself in the most convincing way ever.

If you have negative self-talk or other thoughts come up, capture them down below. Tell your mind, "thank you for that thought" and then let it go. State your identity again.

_____

_____

_____

_____

_____

_____

_____

_____

_____

_____

Repeat the process until you are 100% congruent with the identity and the negative thoughts stop.

☐ As a follow up exercise, take any negative thoughts that may have come up and reframe them into the positive, new affirmations, *"saying, thinking, feeling and seeing yourself the way you want to be!"*

_____

_____

_____

_____

_____

_____

☐ Repeat this exercise today as many times as you can.

The Simple Solution: With every thought, idea, decision, feeling or belief, *"BE THE WAY YOU WANT TO BE TODAY!!!"*

I will see you later tonight for the evening exercise.

NOTES:

EVENING #14

Good Evening,

Well, how was your day? How many times did you look in the mirror? If you didn't do the exercise because it was too intense you'll have another opportunity tonight, remember repetition is the mother of all skill so...DO IT! Your new life begins at the edge of your comfort zone!

ARE YOU READY?

☐ Take out your journal or your note card from this morning and get your purposeful identity statement, who you are "BEING." Print it out again on one of your note cards, BIG and legible.

I,*(your name)*_____

am being _____

☐ Take your note card into your bathroom (you'll need a mirror), or in a private place, along with this book and your journal.

☐ Next, memorize your Identity and look deep into your eyes in the mirror. Repeat your identity to yourself in the most convincing way ever.

If you have negative self-talk or other thoughts come up, capture them down below. Tell your mind, "thank you for that thought" and then let it go. State your identity again.

_____

_____

_____

_____

Repeat the process until you are 100% congruent with the identity and the negative thoughts stop.

☐ As a follow up exercise, take any negative thoughts from that may have come up and reframe them into the positive, new affirmations, *"saying, thinking, feeling and seeing yourself the way you want to be!"*

_____

_____

_____

_____

_____

_____

☐ Repeat this exercise tonight as many times as it takes.

The Simple Solution: With every thought, idea, decision, feeling or belief, *"BE THE WAY YOU WANT TO BE TODAY!!!"*

☐ Repeat your identity and, *"BE the way you want to BE."* Picture yourself 'BE-ing' how you want to BE as you fall asleep in bed.

See you tomorrow for Day #15.

61

DAY #15
IT'S BEEN **2** WEEKS...AMAZING!

Good Morning! Today is a MASTERY REVIEW of our first two weeks together. Grab a cup of water, coffee or juice and let's take a stroll down memory lane.

MASTERY REVIEW:

Your only place of Power is right NOW!

The Simple Solution: With every thought, idea, decision, feeling or belief, *"SEE, HEAR, FEEL AND SAY IT THE WAY YOU WANT IT TO BE!"*

What you have in your life now is the sum total of all of your conscious and unconscious thoughts and decisions you have made to date.

Space needs to be made for new thoughts and beliefs. Make that space by being willing to give up old thoughts and habits of thinking.

The mind does not register the word, 'not.'

Use it in a fun way to 'not' remember that using these skills can be fun and produce results easily and effortlessly.

Expand from not only saying it, but also *"thinking, feeling and seeing your life the way you want it to be!"*

No one builds the foundations under their dreams alone, ask for help.

If you are practicing *"saying it the way you want it to be"* you are drastically reducing talking to yourself and others about your problems and challenges.

Resistance happens because we have been working to change your beliefs by, *"saying it the way you want it to be!"* However, at a deeper level those new beliefs may not match your deeper core identity.

People eventually have to change to adapt their actions to who they believe themselves to be in their core identity.

We all go through 4-Rungs of the Learning Ladder: UI-Unconsciously Incompetent, UC-Unconsciously Competent, CC-Consciously Competent & Finally UC-Unconsciously Competent.

People code their experiences with visual, auditory or kinesthetic cues.

Looking either up and to the right or left will either recall or construct/create pictures easily in our minds.

Visualizing pictures in our mind is easy once we discover our personal pattern.

Reinforce visualization by getting the picture you want to create and sliding it down right in front of your mind.

A purposeful person stays focused on building and creating a meaningful emotional experience that will empower others to build and create theirs.

Being purposeful puts you in a place of power. There is *power in purpose*. It creates motivation, excitement, determination and a feeling of greatness.

There is purpose in your long term goals, especially the ones that are scary/terrify you and fear is present!

Fear prevents most people from achieving what they really want in life.

Fear has many derivative states: scared, anxious, insecure, doubtful, panicked, alarmed, hesitant or mistrusting.

Fear and excitement are the two most closely linked physiological emotional states.

Courage, Faith and Trust are keys to shifting from fear to excitement.

Fear comes from seeing, thinking and feeling an end outcome the way you 'don't' want it to be!

Change happens in the correct order of Being-Doing-Having.

Identity is ESSENTIAL for long-term, empowering change. How you SEE yourself is extremely important.

The Simple Solution: With every thought, idea, decision, feeling or belief, ***"SAY IT THE WAY YOU WANT IT TO BE!"***

Today's Exercise:

☐ Continue to state your purposeful identity statement in the mirror, capturing any negative thoughts, and reframing them into affirmations.

☐ As you move through the day, consistently ask, "Is the task I am engaged in building and creating towards my purposeful life?" If so, continue, if not, readjust to what will.

☐ Practice the rest of the day, *"say it the way you want it to be!"*

NOTES:

EVENING #15

Good Evening,

Well, how was your day? Hopefully, just as you wanted it to be.

☐ Review the mastery materials from this morning and say them **OUT LOUD**.

☐ Continue to state your purposeful identity statement in the mirror, capturing any negative thoughts, and reframing them into affirmations.

☐ Get excited about tomorrow, we start putting this all to work into a goal setting program!

☐ Write out tomorrow, BEing the way you want it to BE tomorrow. Picture yourself BEing that person tomorrow as you fall asleep in bed.

See you tomorrow for Day #16.

NOTES:

DAY #16
BUILDING YOUR LIFE PLAN

Today we start building your Dynamic Life Plan! I'm excited, so let's get down to it!

Today is Purpose Day! We are going to build your Dynamic Life Plan with a 'top down' approach. Becoming fully associated to your purpose should always be the start of your day. It defines the pinnacle of your personal achievement, the height of your glory and the meaning for your life.

Earlier, we talked about purpose as being your answer to the question, "What can I build or create in my life that is emotionally fulfilling for me and will motivate and inspire others to do the same?" Remember the one thing a person has to fight their entire life is entropy.

Today's Exercise:

☐ Take out your Journal and write your Purpose! (refer back to Day #9)

_____

_____

☐ Next, write your answer to the following question, "What is most important to me in my life?"

Keep writing about 2 pages until you run out of words 3 times or start to repeat what you are writing 3 times.

_____

_____

_____

_____

☐ "What is most important to me in my life?" (continued)

_____

_____

_____

_____

_____

_____

_____

_____

_____

_____

_____

_____

_____

_____

_____

_____

_____

_____

☐ "What is most important to me in my life?" (continued)

_____

_____

_____

_____

_____

_____

_____

_____

_____

_____

_____

_____

_____

_____

_____

_____

_____

_____

☐ Pull out your values from what you just wrote. Values are words that capture our emotions like love, happiness, achievement, power, strength, freedom and they can also be emotions like worry, anxiety, fear, sadness and guilt (if you would like some help, refer to Appendix A for a list of values).

_____

_____

_____

_____

☐ List any negative values that came up and reframe them to, *"say it the way you want it to be!"*

_____

_____

_____

_____

☐ Next, take all of your values and condense them into your top 5!

1.

2.

3.

4.

5.

These Top 5 Life Values represent the emotions that you value the most in life.

Pick one of your top 5 Life values and write it here. _____

Close your eyes and look up and to the right or left to your visual construct/create. Mentally walk through your day visualizing yourself feeling more of that value. Picture it as clear as you can. Make the picture bigger and brighter as you *"see, hear and feel"* more of it through throughout your day today.

Ask yourself, "How can I continue to live with more _____today? (insert your life value)"

☐ Continue **The Simple Solution:** With every thought, idea, decision, feeling or belief, *"SAY IT THE WAY YOU WANT IT TO BE!"*

The rest of the exercise will be this evening!

NOTES:

EVENING #16

Good Evening,

Well, how was your day? Amazing, I hope you are continuing to ***"say it the way you want it to be!"***

This evenings exercise is a simple brainstorm.

☐ Rewrite your top 5 Life Values.

1.

2.

3.

4.

5.

Answer each of the following questions.

☐ What are all the things I could Be, Do or Have in my Life that would allow me to feel or experience more _____? (insert Value #1)

_____

_____

_____

_____

☐ What are all the things I could Be, Do or Have in my Life that would allow me to feel or experience more _____? (insert Value #2)

_____

_____

_____

_____

_____

☐ What are all the things I could Be, Do or Have in my Life that would allow me to feel or experience more _____? (insert Value #3)

_____

_____

_____

_____

_____

☐ What are all the things I could Be, Do or Have in my Life that would allow me to feel or experience more _____? (insert Value #4)

_____

_____

_____

_____

_____

☐ What are all the things I could Be, Do or Have in my Life that would allow me to feel or experience more _____? (insert Value #5)

_____

_____

_____

_____

_____

You now have a potential list of goals! They could be 1, 3, 5, 10, 20 year or lifetime goals. Take a look at them. Which ones speak to your emotions the most? Which ones do you feel the greatest anticipation or anxiety towards? Which ones do you fear the most? These are the ones that will be the most meaningful for you to achieve.

_____

☐ List a few that excite you or are the most scary for you to accomplish.

_____

_____

_____

_____

☐ Pick one of your top ideas and practice, *"seeing it the way you want it to be!"* in your mind as you fall asleep!

See you tomorrow for Day #17.

NOTES:

DAY #17
WHAT DO YOU VALUE?

Good Morning! Wow, yesterday was a little bit of writing wasn't it! Well, most people never get this introspective, so if it was challenging then you did it correctly. Today is going to be a little easier on you.

Now...in this moment...NOW...is Power. In your thinking, feeling, seeing, and believing in a better future for yourself...the only power you will ever have to create that life, habit or thinking pattern, is in this very moment...NOW. The power to create that better life now is harnessed through out emotions.

We have sub-value systems for different areas of our life. If you think about your life as a Table of Contents, it would look like this.

MY LIFE (defined value system, Top 5 in Day #16)

I. Physical Health/Wellness

II. Job/Career

III. Relationships

IV. Finances

V. Emotional Health

VI. Spirituality

Today's Exercise:

Develop your top 5 values list for every sub-area of your life. If they come out as stated in the negative remember to ***"RE-WRITE IT THE WAY YOU WANT IT TO BE!"***

I. Physical Health/Wellness

    1. _____
    2. _____
    3. _____
    4. _____
    5. _____

II. Job/Career

    1. _____
    2. _____
    3. _____
    4. _____
    5. _____

III. Relationships

    1. _____
    2. _____
    3. _____
    4. _____
    5. _____

IV. Finances

1. _____
2. _____
3. _____
4. _____
5. _____

V. Emotional Health

1. _____
2. _____
3. _____
4. _____
5. _____

VI. Spirituality

1. _____
2. _____
3. _____
4. _____
5. _____

☐ Next, take all of your values from the sub-areas and condense them into your top 5!

1.

2.

3.

4.

5.

Pick one of your top 5 values from your sub-areas and write it here. _____

Close your eyes and look up and to the right or left to your visual construct/create. Mentally walk through your day visualizing yourself feeling more of that value. Picture it as clear as you can. Make the picture bigger and brighter as you *"see, hear and feel"* more of it through throughout your day today.

Ask yourself, "How can I continue to live with more _____today? (insert your life value)"

I will see you later tonight for this evening's exercise.

EVENING #17

Good Evening,

Well, how was your day? Did you *"see, hear and feel"* more of the value that you chose earlier? Did you practice, *"saying it the way you wanted it to be?"*

☐ Tonight review your life values (Day #16) and this morning's sub-area values. How do you feel about them. Make any necessary adjustments in your lists until they feel right.

☐ Pick your #1 life value _____

and picture yourself Being-Doing-Having and LIVING it in your life tomorrow as you fall asleep in bed.

☐ Write out your day tomorrow, *"seeing, hearing and feeling it the way you want it to be!"*

_____

_____

_____

See you tomorrow for Day #18.

NOTES:

DAY #18
PERSONAL VALUES

Good Morning! Today is going to be simple. Grab a cup of water, coffee or juice and let's get down to business.

☐ **The Simple Solution:** With every thought, idea, decision, feeling or belief, ***"SAY IT THE WAY YOU WANT IT TO BE!"*** Think of something that you want to have or achieve today. Visualize (look up to the right or left) it happening today!

Today's Exercise:

Brainstorm for each of the following questions. Take the first three sets of values; Physical Health/Wellness, Job/Career and Relationships and answer the following questions.

☐ What are all the things I could do in my *Physical Health/Wellness* that would allow me to feel or experience more_____?(insert Health Values #1)

_____

_____

_____

_____

_____

_____

_____

_____

_____

_____

_____

_____

_____

_____

☐ What are all the things I could do in my _Job/Career_ that would allow me to feel or experience more_____? (insert Job/Career Values #2)

_____

_____

_____

_____

_____

_____

_____

_____

_____

_____

_____

_____

_____

_____

☐ What are all the things I could do in my _Relationships_ that would allow me to feel or experience more_____? (insert Relationship Values #3)

_____

_____

_____

_____

_____

_____

_____

_____

_____

_____

_____

_____

_____

You now have a potential list of goals in your physical health/wellness, job/career & relationship categories! They could be 1, 3, 5, 10, 20 year or lifetime goals. Take a look at them. Which ones speak to your emotions the most? Which ones do you feel the greatest anticipation or anxiety towards? Which ones do you fear the most? These are the goals that will be the most meaningful for you to achieve.

_____

_____

☐ Pick one and write it out the *"way you want it to be!"*

_____

_____

I will see you later tonight for the evening exercise.

EVENING #18

Good Evening,

Tonight review your brainstormed ideas/goals. Do any of them move and inspire you? Pick one from each area of life that you would like to accomplish in the next three, six, or twelve months.

I. Physical Health/Wellness

_____

_____

II. Job/Career

_____

_____

III. Relationships

_____

_____

☐ **OUT LOUD** say each thing you want, *"saying it the way you want it to be!"* Visualize in your visual construct/create a very clear and concise picture of the very last thing that needs to happen in order for you to know that you have achieved it.

☐ Picture yourself having them one by one as you fall asleep in bed.

See you tomorrow for Day #19.

DAY #19
PERSONAL VALUES (CONT'D)

Good Morning! Today we are finishing up values for the second set of personal values. Grab a cup of water, coffee or juice and let's go.

☐ **The Simple Solution:** With every thought, idea, decision, feeling or belief, ***"SAY IT THE WAY YOU WANT IT TO BE!"*** Think of something that you want to have or achieve today. Visualize (look up to the right or left) it happening today!

Today's Exercise:

Brainstorm for each of the following questions. Take your values from the second three sets of values; Finances, Emotional Health and Spiritual Life (Day #17) and answer the following questions.

☐ What are all the things I could do in my *Finances* that would allow me to feel or experience

more_____? (insert Finance Values #4)

_____

_____

_____

_____

_____

_____

_____

_____

_____

_____

_____

_____

_____

☐ What are all the things I could do for my *Emotional Health* that would allow me to feel or experience more_____? (insert Emotional Values #5)

_____

_____

_____

_____

_____

_____

_____

_____

_____

_____

_____

_____

_____

_____

☐ What are all the things I could do for my *Spiritual Health* that would allow me to feel or experience more_____? (insert Spiritual Values #6)

_____

_____

_____

_____

_____

_____

_____

_____

_____

_____

_____

_____

_____

_____

You now have a potential list of goals for you in your financial, emotional health & spiritual categories! They could be 1, 3, 5, 10, 20 year or lifetime goals. Take a look at them. Which ones speak to your emotions the most? Which ones do you feel the greatest anticipation or anxiety towards? Which ones do you fear the most? These are the goals that will be the most meaningful for you to achieve.

_____

_____

☐ Pick one and write it out the *"way you want it to be!"*

_____

_____

I will see you later tonight for the evening exercise.

EVENING #19

Good Evening,

Tonight review your brainstormed ideas/goals. Do any of them move and inspire you? Pick one from each area of life that you would like to accomplish in the next three, six, or twelve months.

IV. Finances

_____

_____

V. Emotional Health

_____

_____

VI. Spiritual Life

_____

_____

☐ **OUT LOUD** say each thing you want, ***"saying it the way you want it to be!"*** Visualize in your visual construct/create a very clear and concise picture of the very last thing that needs to happen in order for you to know that you have achieved it.

☐ Picture yourself having them one by one as you fall asleep in bed.

See you tomorrow for Day #20.

DAY #20
THE DONUT

Good Morning! This morning we are going to have a Donut with our coffee!

Remember, values represent a deep feeling inside that we want more of or don't think that we have enough of. Some values we really want to move towards, like love, joy, happiness and fun.
Some values we will do anything to stay away from like anger, sadness, fear, guilt, shame, or anxiety.

There are different sets of values for each area of life. On Day #4, we talked about the power of identity. Values define our identity and ultimately to help us become a person that lives their value system.

If values are closely linked to identity, then setting goals based on value systems will naturally reinforce our identity. Similarly, if a person has to act in accordance with their identity, then they will act based on their value systems and will be more motivated and emotionally associated to their achieving their goals.

So, today we are going to take a break on writing and just review our values. And, of course, remember:

The <u>Simple Solution:</u> With every thought, idea, decision, feeling or belief, ***"SAY IT THE WAY YOU WANT IT TO BE!"***

Today's Exercise:

☐ Fill out the 'donut' template in Appendix B. Insert your life values from Day #16 and your life category values from Day #17 into the template. Copy the 'donut' and carry it around with you.

☐ Review it throughout the day. Ask yourself, "How can I live with more _____ today? (insert the appropriate value into each area of your life).

Work to *live* your values as much as possible, ***"the way you want it to be!"***

EVENING #20

Good Evening,

Well, how was your day? Take out your 'donut' again and look at your values.

☐ Pick one of your Life values and write it here. _____

Close your eyes and look up and to the right or left to your visual construct/create. Visualize how your day tomorrow will be with more of that life value. How would that look? Make the pictures bigger and brighter as you *"see, hear and feel"* more of it in your life.

Ask yourself, "How can I live with more _____tomorrow? (insert your life value)

☐ Work to visualize any other life values or specific category values in your day tomorrow, *"the way you want it to be!"*

See you tomorrow for Day #21.

NOTES:

DAY #21
THE PECKING ORDER

Good Morning! Can you believe it...we are over two thirds of the way done! Congratulations!

You should have in your notes now: Your values 'Donut' page, and 7 pages (1 for your life and 1 for each sub-area of life) of possible things you could Be, Do and Have that would allow you to have more _____in your _____!

Today, let's start to put the puzzle together. These BIG and small possible goals should be prioritized and broken down into possible time frames for your future.

Today's Exercise:

☐ Review All of your life goals and category goals from days #16, 18 & 19 from each day's brainstorm List.

☐ Label the goals for their appropriate time completion. Are they 1, 2, 3, 5, 10, 15 or 20 year goals?

Think of this like putting together a puzzle. How do they fit together so you are happy and balanced completing them, as well as managing all the volume of time, energy and effort it will take to accomplish them. (ie, starting a business, writing a book, having a baby, completing an Ironman Triathlon, moving into a new house and becoming debt free may be just a bit too much for one calendar year)

☐ Write down your top LIFE goal and ONE goal for each of your categories that you want to accomplish in the next year.

LIFE: _____

_____

_____

I. Physical Health/Wellness

_____

_____

II. Job/Career

_____

_____

III. Relationships

_____

_____

IV. Finances

_____

_____

V. Emotional Health

_____

_____

VI. Spiritual Life

_____

_____

☐ Continue with **The Simple Solution:** pick a value you want to experience the most today and take a moment to visualize it several times throughout the rest of the day, *"the way you want it to be!"*

EVENING #21

Good Evening, things should be getting exciting now as you move towards defining more of your specific goals. Is your future getting clearer? I hope so!

☐ Go back to day #9 (p. 29) and find your purpose statement. Re-write it below.

_____

_____

_____

☐ Review your 1-year goals from Day #20. Make sure they are congruent with your purpose statement.

☐ Pick one and practice *"seeing it the way you want it to be!"* as you fall asleep!

See you tomorrow for Day #22, where we will get S.M.A.R.T. about our goals!

NOTES:

DAY #22
LET'S GET **S.M.A.R.T.** ABOUT IT!

Today we are going to keep things S.M.A.R.T.! Yes, perhaps you have heard of this acronym before when people start to talk about goals. There is a good reason for that but it is only half of the equation for true goal attainment. Let's get to it!

Reading:

One of the little known facts about achieving any goal is that there are actually 2 parts of the brain that need to be synchronized together: the right brain and left brain.

The right brain is all about emotions while the left brain is all about the facts, figures, and logic. Today, we are going to explore the left side of the brain, the analytical part.

The S.M.A.R.T. acronym in goal setting is for the left brain. In order for the goal to make sense for the left brain it needs to meet the parameters of S.M.A.R.T. They are:

S = **S**imple and **S**pecific (so that a 7 year old would understand)

M = **M**easureable and **M**eaningful to you (goal for you, not someone else)

A = **A**ction Oriented and stated **A**s-If Now (stated like it has been completed)

R = **R**easonable and **R**ealistic (goals must push you outside of your comfort zone yet still be within a persons realm of possibility, i.e. - I can't be a pro golfer at 45 never having picked up a club before)

T = **T**ime included and **T**owards what you want (said the way you want it to be in the positive sense)

A *non*-S.M.A.R.T. goal is: "I want to complete and run a marathon someday and not get injured."

A S.M.A.R.T. goal is: "I have successfully completed the NYC Marathon on November 3, 2013 in 5 hours or less, injury free."

Notice: if you do this correctly, your goals will be logical, nice, neat and measureable. They will also be devoid of any emotion because they are left brained and measurable! This is what provides clarity, focus and direction.

Today's Exercise:

☐ Write your Top LIFE goal and category goals for the next year in the S.M.A.R.T. format.

LIFE: _____

_____

_____

I. Physical Health/Wellness

_____

_____

II. Job/Career

_____

_____

III. Relationships

_____

_____

IV. Finances*

_____

_____

V. Emotional Health

_____

_____

VI. Spiritual Life

_____

_____

☐ Continue with **<u>The Simple Solution:</u>** pick a VALUE from your top 5 life values, you want to experience the most today and take a moment to visualize what it would look like if you lived it throughout the rest of the day, *"the way you want it to be!"*

*A note on your financial goal. Remember that Purpose is about building and creating. If your financial goal is a dollar amount, i.e. "I have made $150,000 on or before December 31, 2014." It would be better to set your goal by answering, "What am I going to build and create on or before December 31, 2014 that will allow me to receive $150,000 or more in return?" Money is a great measurement tool to assess your progress but it is better to focus on building and creating or incorporating the two. i.e., "I have built a superior coaching practice with 60 active clients, an online membership site and written two books on or before December 31, 2014 which generate over $150,000 in annual revenue."

NOTES:

EVENING #22

Good Evening,

How was your day? Did you gain a different perspective as you remembered your 1-year goals?

☐ Review your S.M.A.R.T. goals and refine them as needed into better S.M.A.R.T. goals.

☐ Review and visualize each one, *"seeing them the way you want them to be!"*

☐ Picture yourself having them one by one as you fall asleep in bed.

See you tomorrow for Day #23 when we define and integrate the right brain process for goal setting.

NOTES:

DAY #23
THE VERY LAST THING

Good Morning! Today's morning routine is learning how to engage the right side of your brain in the goals process. Grab a cup of water, coffee or juice and let's go!

First, review your S.M.A.R.T. goals from yesterday. As you read them, are they devoid of emotion? Remember we are engaging the left brain. Do you remember my example? "I have successfully completed the NYC marathon on November 3, 2013 in 5 hours or less, injury free?" It is a clearly focused, analytical, measureable left brain goal.

To engage the right brain, we ask, **"What is the very last thing that needs to happen in order for me to know I have achieved this goal?"** This is where you generate the pictures, thoughts, and most importantly, feelings and emotions of, *"the way you want it to be."*

My answer, "I see myself running the last 100-yards of the race, a slight breeze on my cheeks as the crowd cheers in Central Park. I look to the left and see my wife in the stands clapping and cheering for me. Looking up I see the official race clock at 4:24:37 and hear the beep of my timing chip as I cross the line, feeling elated, euphoric and triumphant. I smile ear to ear as the volunteer puts the medal around my neck and I see on the medal, "NYC Marathon, Nov 3, 2013" and think to myself, "I DID IT!"

This last answer carries emotion! Everything in the S.M.A.R.T. goal is incorporated into my picture and it paints a great emotionally charged visualization of the very last thing.

Remember one of our initial exercises was to practice visualization of our goals? This is what I start to picture in my mind as I go to sleep every night. This very last thing exercise integrates every skill we have been working on developing over the course of the last 21 days. It is **The Simple Solution** of *"saying, seeing and feeling it the way we want it to be,"*

WOW! Now we have fully harnessed the power of our mind to create an incredible reality! I hope, this is powerful moment for you! Do you see the process now of how greatness is created. Andre Agassi was asked what it felt like, after winning Wimbledon for the first time, and he answered, "I have been picturing this moment since I was a child and it feels just the same as all of the other times I imagined it."

YOU have now harnessed the power to create MAGIC just like Andre did! I hope you feel incredible right now!

Today's Exercise:

☐ **The Simple Solution:** With every thought, idea, decision, feeling or belief, *"SAY IT THE WAY YOU WANT IT TO BE!"*

☐ Take your S.M.A.R.T. goals and for each one of them, ask yourself, "What is the very last thing that needs to happen in order for me to know that I have achieved this goal?" Have your answers be full of emotions, times, dates, thoughts, feelings and pictures.

Really engage **The Simple Solution** and *"see, hear, think, feel and say it the way you want it to be!"* Make sure your emotional association is at 100%.

LIFE: _____

_____

_____

_____

_____

_____

I. Physical Health/Wellness

_____

_____

_____

_____

_____

II. Job/Career

_____

_____

_____

_____

_____

_____

III. Relationships

_____

_____

_____

_____

_____

_____

IV. Finances

_____

_____

_____

_____

_____

_____

V. Emotional Health

_____

_____

_____

_____

_____

_____

VI. Spiritual Life

_____

_____

_____

_____

_____

_____

☐ Pick one of your top goal(s) and visualize them!

I will see you later tonight for the evening exercise.

EVENING #23

Good Evening,

A lot of work today! And hopefully you are energized with all of this positive feeling and emotion you have created!

This evenings exercise is a continuation of this morning.

☐ Finish up the rest of your S.M.A.R.T. goals by completing the right brain pictures to them.

☐ Visualize each goal, *"saying it the way you want it to be!"* **OUT LOUD.** Picture yourself and the very last thing that has to happen in order for you to know you have achieved it, one by one as you fall asleep in bed.

See you tomorrow for Day #24.

NOTES:

DAY #24
PASS ME THE CATCH-UP!

Good Morning! Today is a Catch-Up day! Grab a cup of water, coffee or juice and let's review.

We have done a lot of work in the last 10 days. We have uncovered your life purpose, your deep values (feelings that drive behaviors), learned to brainstorm goals based on these values, picked a few of them and learned to engage them with the left brain (S.M.A.R.T. goals), and the right brain (emotions-what's the very last thing?).

All of this was done with a positive, forward thinking mental focus thanks to **The Simple Solution**, *"THINKING, FEELING, SEEING AND SAYING IT THE WAY YOU WANT YOUR LIFE TO BE!"*

Today's Exercise:

Today is a Catch-Up day. Review and complete if necessary:

☐ Your purpose statement and values donut

☐ Your 1-Year life and category goals. If any are not completed, finish writing them in the S.M.A.R.T. format. Follow up and write the very last thing you need to happen in order for you to know you have achieved your goal for each one.

☐ Add in **The Simple Solution** and visualize yourself, *"seeing, hearing, thinking and feeling the very last thing the way you want it to be!"*

☐ It has been a lot of work the last few days! **Catch-Up!** If there is anything that is missing from the past few days, complete the exercises.

EVENING #24

Good Evening,

This evenings exercise is simple...continue to Catch-Up for the day!

☐ Catch-Up and Review!

☐ Write a few very last thing moments out and say them **OUT LOUD.**

_____

_____

_____

_____

_____

_____

_____

_____

_____

☐ Visualize yourself completing your goals one by one as you fall asleep.

See you tomorrow for Day #25.

DAY #25
THE POWER OF ASSOCIATION

Good Morning! Up to this point we have worked on everything that is going on inside of your mind. Do you remember that I told you when we started that my outcome was to shift your thinking? Over the last 24 Days of work that is exactly what we have been working to master. You have completed the hardest work in achieving the life of your dreams. We are now going to shift our attention to the external world. Let's get to work!

If you think of a room in your house and all of the 'things' that are in it, each one carries an emotional connection. An interesting note about people's 'things' is that they are all items from the past.

As I look around my office, everything has a emotional connection and memory _to the past_. There are three different emotional connections that a 'thing' can have: positive, neutral or negative. Over time, our emotional connection with our 'things' can change.

Think about this seriously for a moment. For the last 24 days we have created a clear mental picture of what you want to have and achieve.

Today's Exercise:

☐ Close your eyes and visualize that for a moment (looking up and to your right or left) your goal.

Now, as you look around the room is there anything that positively reinforces what you want to build and create? Every material possession has an emotional attachment. Be careful because sometimes the emotional representations also change over time.

Example: Do you remember that stuffed bear or gift you gave, or got, from your first love? At first, it represented nothing but deep feeling of love and connection, right? And then what happened to the emotional connection the bear had after the big, heart wrenching break up?

☐ First, put your head down, slump your shoulders, breathe really shallow and think of your first love dumping you and being heartbroken. Now, in this poor state, scan the room you are in and write down what you notice. (chances are it will be things that are negative to neutral in emotional connection)

_____

_____

☐ Next, put your shoulders back, chin up above parallel to the floor, think and remember bright happy thoughts, and scan the room. What do you see now in this great state that is different than before? What makes you happy?

_____

_____

☐ Think of your goals and compare your picture of the very last thing to achieve with the 'things' in your room. Take out one material item or possession that does not support the very last thing with your goals.

☐ What is the item that you chose to let go of? _____

☐ What feelings are or were attached to it initially? _____

☐ How do you feel about it now? _____

Some things may be hard to let go of, but in the end, letting go of those negative associations will be very beneficial.

EVENING #25

Good Evening,

Well, how are you feeling in your room? Do you miss the items you purged that didn't relate to your goal? If so, what did the object represent? What emotion did it allow you to feel or experience? What value?

☐ Review your goals and clear out one or two more things that carry a negative or disempowering emotional connection. What emotions did you have for them initially and what emotions are present now?

_____

_____

☐ Say thank you and good bye to all of the things that were negative and you removed.

☐ Review your goals and last things for your visualization exercises at bedtime.

☐ *"Say them the way you want them to be!"* **OUT LOUD.** Picture yourself having them one by one as you fall asleep in bed.

See you tomorrow for Day #26.

NOTES:

DAY #26
CLEAR YOUR CLUTTER

Good Morning! Today we are going to raise the bar on clearing the clutter.

Yesterday, we learned that every 'thing' in your life has an emotional association that is either positive, negative or neutral. Over time, these emotional associations can change unconsciously.

Today we are going to do a MASSIVE clear your clutter party. I would challenge you to immediately scan your house and take out everything that is negative or neutral in its emotional association.

I did this in my office about a year ago. I literally took everything out of my office except for my chair, phone, desk and computer. I took everything off of the walls, took all of the trinkets and treasures away and cleared out everything from my supply closet.

Everything went into supply boxes that ended up lining up nicely in the hallway to my office. As I moved through the next couple of weeks I only took back into the office what was useful. Everything else ended up in the garage for 3 months. Eventually, I went through it one more time and then it either went into the trash or Goodwill.

The main outcome of this purging of 'things' was to create emptiness. The outcome is to let go of everything from the past and create a new open, uncluttered, empty space.

It is best for you to decide how to handle this. I would suggest one room at a time. The more you can clear and create open space the better. Tomorrow we will talk about the importance of creating emptiness in the pursuit of your goals. This will really stretch you, and I encourage you to face it with courage.

Today's Exercise:

☐ Remember **The Simple Solution:** With every thought, idea, decision, feeling or belief, ***"SAY IT THE WAY YOU WANT IT TO BE!"***

☐ Pick one room in your house. During the day today, empty it of everything except for what is absolutely critical. Empty every drawer, cabinet, closet, shelf, cubby and space. If it's junk, into the trashcan it goes!

109

☐ Or, you can box everything up for Goodwill. If you donate your items, make sure and let these 'things' go freely and voluntarily. Thank them for their usefulness over the years and let them go to someone who will really want or need them. They will live on with a positive emotional association for the other person. Remember, one person's junk is another person's treasure.

☐ If you can't bear to purge your room of the items that have a negative emotional association, pack the items away in boxes or tubs in the garage, attic or basement. If you need something, bring it back into the room, otherwise, let it go. After 3-6 months if you have not used the stuff, let it go!

☐ Review your values donut, goals and very last things.

I will see you later tonight for the evening exercise.

NOTES:

EVENING #26

Good Evening,

How are you doing sitting in your place of emptiness? Tonight is catch-up time. If you have not cleaned out the clutter, pick a space in your home/office and DO IT NOW! If you are pushing up against any resistance then remember that it is a good thing to release negative associations and objects.

☐ If you didn't get the one room cleared out, continue on until it is complete.

Sit in your place of emptiness and notice if it is more comfortable or uncomfortable, write out how you feel. Reinforce any positive feelings and write down any uncomfortable feelings.

_____

_____

_____

_____

☐ Review your goals and rewrite them while *"saying it the way you want it to be!"* **OUT LOUD.** Continue to visualize yourself having them one by one as you fall asleep in bed.

_____

_____

_____

_____

See you tomorrow for Day #27.

DAY #27
BE FULL OF EMPTINESS

Good Morning! I hope that you are sitting down in an empty room today and it feels a little 'weird!'

In the book, "The 12 Conditions of a Miracle," Todd Michaels states that creating emptiness is the first condition present for a miracle to happen. Before any change can happen, new space needs to be created. This new space should be seen as emptiness. Emptiness can be both internal with our thoughts and feelings and external with our material possessions and environment.

Let's illustrate this concept with a few examples. Let's say a young woman has recently broken up with her boyfriend and now wishes to get back into another serious relationship.

During her healing time, she started to let the dog and cat sleep in bed with her at night so she wasn't alone. She also went out and bought a long body pillow so she could feel cozy in bed at night and not miss someone else being there.

If she truly wanted a new relationship and it wasn't happening, I would coach her to get the dog, cat and pillow out of the bed. In an extreme case, get a new mattress, sheets and pillow too! These new items would be free of any old unconscious negative patterns and memories, and create in her environment the empty 'space' to be filled.

For a guy in a similar situation, I may recommend that he clear out 2/3 of the closet to make space for his new girlfriends clothes, get a second toothbrush, some women's shampoo for the shower and clean out some drawers in the bathroom vanity.

The reason this works is because nature abhors a vacuum. When there is a space of emptiness, nature will work to fill it. How it is filled in your life is directed by your thoughts. That is why it is key to, *"see, hear and feel your life the way you want it to be!"* Nature will fill your space by what your thoughts tell it to.

One more quick example, when I was 60 lbs overweight and struggling with my weight, I had to learn to enjoy the 'empty' feelings of being hungry. Naturally, I used **The Simple Solution** of *"SAYING IT THE WAY I WANTED IT TO BE,"* by finding a new meaning for hunger.

I would tell myself when I felt hungry, "Now, in this moment, my body really needs water to hydrate and cleanse itself because the fat burning is just starting now and I enjoy the process."

After 20 minutes if the feeling persisted, I would eat the healthiest choice I could find. The hardest thing to do was sit with the feelings of emptiness in my stomach and find a new belief *"saying it the way I wanted it to be!"* But, that was also the moment I pictured the guy in the Dr. Pepper commercial in jeans and white t-shirt! The result? I kept running, eating healthy and left 60 lbs behind me, returning to my normal body weight.

Of course, these changes and emptiness will be uncomfortable at first, but take heart, remember that nature does not like a vacuum. Your space will be filled by what you consistently focus on, add emotion to and take action towards, *"saying, feeling and seeing your life the way you want it to be!"*

Today's Exercise:

☐ Today, continue to clear clutter and speak about the new feelings of emptiness *"the way you want it to be."* Continue to create 'space' or 'emptiness' in regards to each of your goals.

☐ In those moments of being uncomfortable, write the feelings of 'emptiness' *"the way you want them to be!"* like I did for the feelings of hunger.

_____

_____

_____

☐ Add into that moment of 'emptiness' and new feelings, the visualization of how it will look when the 'emptiness' is filled with the very last thing that needs to happen in order for you to know you have achieved your goal! (for example, sit in the empty garage and picture the new car you want to have filling that space. Put a picture on the wall and imagine it as real).

_____

_____

_____

I will see you later tonight for the evening exercise.

Evening #27

Good Evening,

Well, how was the empty day? Did you practice enjoying emptiness? Talking to yourself, *"the way you wanted it to be,"* and visualizing the very last thing that needed to happen in order for you to know you have achieved the goal?

When you had empty feelings did you practice finding new ways of how to enjoy that emptiness by **The Simple Solution:** *"SEEING, SAYING AND FEELING IT THE WAY YOU WANT IT TO BE?"*

Tonight, I am going to just brush up on another topic. The last two days have really been about creating external space or emptiness. There is also internal emptiness.

Finding internal emptiness is done through meditation. If you have been doing your visualizations at night, then you are already doing a form of meditation.

☐ Tonight create a space of emptiness inside your mind by closing your eyes, focusing on nothing and calming your mind. If your voice is really loud inside, picture a word in your mind like, "LOVE" or "PEACE" or "RELAX."

Then, focus on the black space in between the words. You will only be able to do it for 1-60 seconds before that internal voice kicks in or your mind wanders. This is normal so just refocus and start again.

☐ Practice holding your attention in emptiness and pay attention to the thoughts and feelings that come. Miraculous things can happen here. You may find solutions to problems, negative feelings disappear, and many other amazing inspirations and intuitions may be provided to you.

☐ Meditate on how you can continue to enjoy emptiness in your life.

☐ Review in your mind your day tomorrow, *"the way you want it to be!"*

114

DAY #28
A NEW PICTURE

Good Morning! For our morning exercise, you will need a blank journal page to draw on.

Today, we are going to explore another way to fill the empty space! Since most of the old material possessions were from the past, we want to put into the empty environment new, meaningful items that represent where we want to go in the future.

For example, if you want to travel, put a world map on the wall with your destinations highlighted. If you want that job promotion, buy a name plaque for your desk with the promotion on it.

Another great tool to fill the emptiness is building a 'wheel of success' from Catherine Ponders book, "The Dynamic Laws of Prosperity."

If we are going to practice **The Simple Solution** and *"SEE, HEAR, THINK AND FEEL MY LIFE THE WAY YOU WANT IT TO BE!"* it would be good to have a visual picture to be able to focus on. You probably also heard of this concept as creating a vision board or collage. This external picture will be a great anchor and reminder of where we are going.

Today's Exercise:

Take out your blank page and do the following:

☐ In the very center of the page, put down your image of Divine Intelligence, God, Jesus or any other picture that represents who you put your faith and trust in to provide for all of your needs. What is your picture of the Divine Intelligence of the Universe?

☐ From the center, split the rest of the page into 4 sections. Each section will represent one of the following areas: Physical Health, Relationships, Money/Finances, and Career.

☐ Put in each space affirmations, pictures that represent the very last thing for each goal, the S.M.A.R.T. goal itself and any other symbol or representation.

☐ Make it as large as you can on a whiteboard, bulletin board or other presentation paper and keep it in your focus at all times.

☐ Make sure that everything on the illustration represents your goals according to **The Simple Solution:** With every thought, idea, decision, feeling or belief, *"SAY IT THE WAY YOU WANT IT TO BE!"*

☐ Create a wheel of success for your life and for you super achievers, every category too.

NOTES:

EVENING #28

Good Evening!

Tonight is Simple. Continue to build your vision board, wheel of happiness or whatever it is that you want to call it. Catch up on any items that you are still behind in. And as always, continue to practice **The Simple Solution**, *"SEEING, HEARING AND FEELING YOUR LIFE THE WAY YOU WANT IT TO BE!"*

☐ Finish the wheel of success for your life and whichever life categories you want.

☐ Write out and visualize your day tomorrow, *"the way you want it to be!"*

_____

_____

_____

_____

_____

_____

☐ Review your goals as you fall asleep and continue to visualize the very last thing that has to happen in order for you to know you have achieved the goal!

See you tomorrow for Day #29. Can you believe we are almost done?

DAY #29
THE 2ND MOST IMPORTANT DAY

Good Morning! The Most Important day of this program was Day #1, where we discovered **The Simple Solution**, ***"SEE, HEAR, FEEL AND THINK YOUR LIFE THE WAY YOU WANT IT TO BE!"***

Today is the ***Second Most Important Day*** of this program and let me explain why.

Do you remember Day #1 and the statement: "Now...in this moment...NOW...is Power. In your thinking, feeling, seeing, and believing in a better future for yourself...the only power you will ever have to create that life, habit or thinking pattern, is in this very moment...NOW?"

Well, for the last 28 days we have been discovering the tools and strategies to shift and change your thinking! That is the first step to achieving any goal; building the belief that you can do it!

Today is the second most important day of this program because now as you use **The Simple Solution** and ***"see, hear, feel and think your life the way you want it to be,"*** we need to add one more thing for it all to work. And that is...

CONGRUENT ACTION day in and day out, plus a healthy dose of TRUST in your outcome becoming real!

It is not just enough to reframe your thinking to ***"see, hear, feel and think your life the way you want it to be,"*** because thinking about a goal doesn't generate emotion. Remember a purposeful person focuses first on building and creating.

If you saw, heard, felt and thought about your ideal mate really hard and sat on the couch every night, well...it's going to be a long time before anyone shows up at the door!

Here's what the movie 'The Secret' never told you! The real 'Secret' is to: ***"see, hear, feel and think your life the way you want it to be,",*** at the exact same time you take ***Congruent Action,*** over and over again!

They conveniently left out the 'taking congruent action' piece because that would not have sold as many videos! People would have said, "what...I have to actually work at it too?" but, now after completing your journey through this book, the hard work is done!

Let's recap all of the NEW TOOLS you have Mastered to *change your thinking.*

CONGRATULATIONS! YOU HAVE SUCCESSFULLY:

☐ Learned <u>The Simple Solution:</u> *"SEEING, HEARING AND FEELING IT THE WAY YOU WANT IT TO BE!"* along with removing negative language patterns like, '<u>not.</u>'

☐ Redefined your <u>Identity.</u> Given yourself a break from perfection with the <u>Learning Ladder</u> and refined your ability to create your future inside by mastering the <u>Art of Visualization.</u>

☐ Discovered <u>Courage</u> and <u>Fearlessness:</u> BE-ing, DO-ing and HAVE-ing more in your life!

☐ Engaged your Emotions that guide your Life and defined your <u>Value Systems.</u>

☐ Brainstormed new <u>Empowering Goals</u> based on your <u>Values,</u> then integrated your left and right brain together by integrating them in the <u>S.M.A.R.T.</u> format and the <u>Very Last Thing.</u>

☐ Last, we learned about the power of <u>Emotional Associations</u> of 'things,' <u>Clearing Clutter</u> to create <u>Emptiness</u> and enhancing our new emptiness with positive <u>Visual Cues</u> (vision boards).

You now have an entire plan for your life, *"the way you want it to be!"* Amazing!

CONGRUENT ACTION is the last ingredient to make this process work. It is the missing element from the 'Secret,' be prepared to take consistent and congruent action while simultaneously using **The Simple Solution** and if you look back in the last 30-Days, I hope that you will see that you have ALREADY DONE THAT!

The Key is to keep your focus on *"how you want it to be in your mind!"* **as you take congruent action!**

Today's Exercise:

☐ Look at your Top Goals. Write down 3-5 specific action items that you are committed to take today while *"seeing, hearing, thinking and feeling it the way you want it to be!"* Imagine that very last thing happening as you take that congruent action!

_____

_____

_____

_____

_____

_____

_____

_____

_____

_____

_____

☐ Patience, persistence and trust will take it from there!

I will see you later tonight for the evening exercise.

EVENING #29

Good Evening,

How did it go today! Did you add congruent action to your thinking? Of course you did! How often were you successful?

☐ Review your one year goals and write down what you are going to accomplish tomorrow. Go through mentally seeing yourself taking the actions and thinking congruently at the same time.

_____

_____

_____

_____

_____

_____

_____

_____

_____

_____

☐ Picture yourself doing them one by one as you fall asleep in bed.

See you tomorrow for Celebration Day #30.

DAY #30
THE END OR THE BEGINNING?

CONGRATULATIONS! You made it 30-Days!

One final question? Is it the end or just the beginning? It could be BOTH!

Where do I suggest you go from here?

☐ **Re-Commit for 30 Days.**

My 30-Day Promise

Today is the first day of the rest of my life. I fully re-commit and promise to persevere in completing this book I have developed in its entirety, starting today.

_____ / _____ / _____

I understand that in order to achieve all that I desire in this life, success lies at managing the risk found at the end of my comfort zone. I strive for excellence and realize that the real work in life begins right at the moment everyone else says they have done enough, quits and goes home. I will stay focused and committed to my word even when they entice me to go with them.

I promise to keep in the front of my mind at all times, **<u>The Simple Solution</u>** and strive to achieve mastery of this one simple principle. I will celebrate my wins and honor my failures, knowing that working through both will lead me to a new life of Success.

I will stand guard at the doorway of my mind and promise to feed it only positive messages mentally, emotionally, physically and spiritually. I will focus on achievement of my goals one day at a time and stay away from looking back over my shoulder to the past or dreaming too far forward into my future. That is where distraction and doubt lie in wait to ambush my success.

To all of this I promise for the next 30 Days, I will put in the time needed to complete this book, Honor my word and respect myself.

I am worthy of the success that I desire!

Signature _____ _____

☐ Then, commit to reviewing the following, *daily*.

☐ My life purpose is to build and create

_____

_____

_____

_____

☐ In order to live my purpose I will strive to live with_____,
_____, _____,
_____ and _____ every day. (life values)

☐ My goals this year are to:

_____

_____

_____

_____

_____

_____

☐ My morning ritual is to visualize and write out my goals, *"the way I want them to be!"*

_____

_____

_____

_____

_____

_____

_____

_____

_____

_____

☐ My evening ritual is to visualize my next day and write out my goals, *"the way I want them to be!"*

_____

_____

_____

_____

☐ I continue to clear my clutter, get comfortable in emptiness and create powerful visual associations in my environment to build and create my life, *"the way I want it to be!"*

_____

_____

_____

_____

_____

_____

_____

_____

_____

EVENING #30

Good Evening,

You have Graduated from the 30-Days for Success program. Pat yourself on the back! Great job!

☐ Write out tomorrow, *"saying it the way you want it to be!"* **OUT LOUD.** Picture yourself continuing to have the life you want to have as you fall asleep in bed.

_____

_____

_____

_____

_____

_____

_____

_____

_____

_____

_____

_____

Congratulations on 30-Days for Success! You are a winner!

BONUS

Continue on with **The Simple Solution:** With every thought, idea, decision, feeling or belief, ***"SAY IT THE WAY YOU WANT IT TO BE!"***

If you have made it this far, you are obviously committed to creating a more empowering life for yourself.

I believe that you are Awesome! I believe in the power of the human spirit, that when unleashed, will change the world!

I wanted to leave you with a quote: Isaiah: 40:25-26

"To whom will you compare me? Or who is my equal?" says the Holy One. Lift your eyes to the heavens: Who created all of these? He who brings out the starry hosts one by one, and calls them each by name. Because of his great power and mighty strength, *not one of them is missing."*

You are unique and special. Share your gift with the world!

To your continued success

James

If you would like to accelerate your results with the benefit of a complimentary 'Success-Now' Session, Call (919) 792-0085 to set up a time.

Mention you have completed the 30-Days for Success book and receive a special Bonus!

APPENDIX A

VALUES LIST

Ability	Abundance	Acceptance	Accomplishment
Achievement	Acknowledgement	Adaptable	Adequate
Adventure	Affection	Affluence	Alert
Alive	Ambition	Amused	Anticipation
Attentive	Attractive	Audacious	Available
Aware	Awe	Balance	Beauty
Being	Belonging	Benevolent	Blissful
Bold	Brave	Brilliant	Brisk
Calm	Camaraderie	Candor	Capable
Caring	Careful	Certainty	Challenge
Charity	Charm	Cheerful	Clarity
Classy	Clean	Clever	Close
Comfort	Commitment	Compassion	Competent
Conform	Congruent	Connection	Consciousness
Consistent	Content	Contribution	Control
Conviction	Cool	Cooperation	Copious
Cordial	Correct	Courage	Courteous
Crafty	Creative	Credibility	Cunning
Curiosity	Daring	Decisive	Deep
Delicate	Delight	Dependable	Depth
Desire	Determination	Devotion	Dignity
Discernment	Discrete	Discipline	Discovery
Eager	Ecstasy	Educated	Effective
Encourage	Endurance	Energy	Enjoyment
Enlightenment	Entertain	Enthusiasm	Exact
Expressive	Evolve	Facilitate	Fair
Faith	Fame	Fascination	Fearless
Fidelity	Finesse	Firm	Fit
Flexible	Flow	Fluent	Fluid
Focus	Fortitude	Freedom	Friendly
Frugal	Fun	Generosity	Gentle
Genuine	Giving	Grace	Grateful
Gratitude	Gregarious	Growth	Guidance
Happiness	Harmony	Health	Helpful
Holy	Honest	Honor	Hope
Hospitable	Humility	Humor	Imagination
Impact	Independent	Industry	Ingenuity
Inquisitive	Insight	Inspiration	Integrity
Intelligence	Intensity	Intimacy	Intuition
Intuitive	Inventive	Joy	Justice

Kind	Knowledgeable	Lavish	Leadership
Learning	Liberty	Lively	Logical
Longevity	Love	Loyal	Mastery
Mature	Meek	Mellow	Meticulous
Mindful	Moderation	Modest	Motivated
Mysterious	Neat	Nerve	Obedient
Open-minded	Open	Optimism	Order
Organized	Original	Outlandish	Outrageousness
Passion	Peace	Perceptive	Perfection
Perseverance	Persistence	Persuasive	Philanthropy
Piety	Playful	Pleasant	Pleasure
Plenty	Poise	Polish	Popular
Potent	Practical	Pragmatic	Precise
Preeminence	Prepared	Present	Privacy
Proactive	Proficient	Professional	Prosper
Prudence	Punctual	Pure	Qualified
Quiet	Quick	Real	Ready
Reason	Recognition	Recreation	Refined
Reflect	Relaxed	Reliable	Resilient
Resolute	Resolve	Resourceful	Respect
Rest	Restraint	Reverence	Rich
Rigor	Sacred	Sacrifice	Satisfaction
Security	Self-control	Selfless	Self-realization
Security	Sensitive	Sensual	Serenity
Service	Sexual	Share	Shrewd
Significance	Silent	Silly	Simple
Sincere	Skillful	Smart	Sophisticated
Solid	Solitude	Sound	Spirit
Spirituality	Spontaneity	Stability	Still
Strength	Structure	Substantial	Success
Sufficient	Support	Surprise	Superb
Supremacy	Sympathy	Synergy	Tactful
Teamwork	Temperance	Thankful	Thorough
Thoughtful	Thrifty	Tidy	Timely
Tradition	Tranquil	Transcendence	Trust
Trustworthiness	Truth	Understanding	Unique
Unite	Useful	Utilize	Valor
Variety	Victory	Vigor	Virtue
Vision	Vital	Vivacious	Warm
Watchful	Wealth	Wholesome	Willing
Winning	Wisdom	Witty	Wonder
Worthy	Zeal	Zest	Zing

Zig Ziglar's Most Common Religious Values

Wisdom ~ Integrity ~ Love ~ Freedom ~ Justice ~ Courage ~ Humility
Patience ~ Industriousness ~ Thriftiness
Generosity ~ Objectivity ~ Optimism ~ Cooperation ~ Moderation

Ben Franklin's Value System

- **Temperance:** not eat to dullness/drink to elevation
- **Silence:** speak only what benefits
- **Order:** all things have a place including time
- **Resolution:** perform what you ought
- **Frugality:** expenses for your benefit & others
- **Industry:** lose not time, employ in usefulness
- **Sincerity:** no hurtful deceits
- **Justice:** wrong none
- **Moderation:** avoid extremes
- **Tranquility:** don't be disturbed by trifles
- **Chastity:** for health or offspring
- **Humility:** imitate Jesus & Socrates

APPENDIX B

THE DONUT

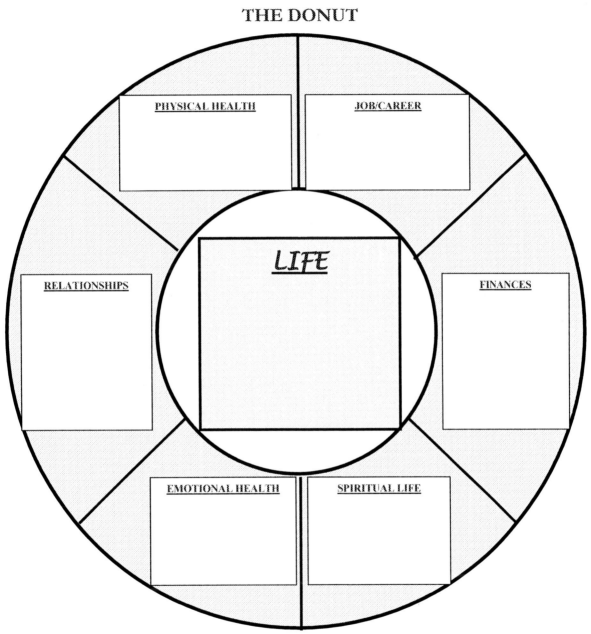

PHYSICAL HEALTH

JOB/CAREER

RELATIONSHIPS

LIFE

FINANCES

EMOTIONAL HEALTH

SPIRITUAL LIFE

What is most Important to me in my _____

NOTES:

JAMES M MURPHY
www.evolutionforsuccess.com
www.30DaysforSuccess.com
www.businessmarketingforsuccess.com
james@evolutionforsuccess.com

About James M Murphy:

James M Murphy has been an Executive Business & Life Coach for the last 15 years. James began with Anthony Robbins Companies as a Peak Performance Results Coach working with entrepreneurs, business owners and executives in 1999.

Through his incredible immersion experience, James' extensive coaching experience dwarfs most coaches in the market today. After conducting over 24,000 sessions, he is a master in the psychology of time management, the entrepreneurial mindset, emotional mastery, goal setting, focus and productivity, problem resolution, communication, money, health and relationships.

James has expanded his skills to include working with clients deeper emotional issues to include release of anxiety, overwhelm, fears and phobias.

James also developed the Sure Hire Employee Evaluation tool which has saved his clients tens of thousands of dollars by hiring the right employees the first time.

FUN FACTS: James just completed his first book, "30-Days for Success," is a certified scuba diver, Mud Run enthusiast, Beach Body Coach™ and Finisher of the Umstead 100-Mile Ultra Marathon.

Looking for a Keynote Speaker?

James has given keynote presentations for companies including General Mills, Dish Network, Walgreens, and the Resource Coaching Academy.

Running Fearless: *Passion, Purpose and Persistence*

Summary of Session:
A new answer to the old question, "How does a leader stay personally motivated and inspire their employees to be the same?" is addressed head on in this dynamic presentation. Motivated employees produce more, are happier, shift an entire business culture and create raving fans. What drives a person to succeed personally and professionally? Better yet, what 3-Finish lines does every business leader need to cross in order to achieve victory? Learn the two time-tested, simple secrets that create a purpose-driven mindset and a proactive thinking method. Find our how to shift your corporate thinking from Impossible to I'm Possible. This is the perfect program to personally and professionally focus on your direction, purpose and outlook. You will leave this program emotionally charged, focused on an empowering future, and motivated to take actions that produce results.

Learning Objectives:
1) Engage employees to come together with one unifying purpose that is emotionally charged, empowering and dynamic
2) Create a purpose driven workforce that trickles down to each individual employee
3) Understand the psychology of goals and achievement in 3 simple steps
4) Provide employees a new paradigm of thinking for their position in the company that will push them to be more engaged and motivated
5) How to adapt and succeed in a rapidly changing company
6) Tools for engaging strategic thinking and leadership into everyday communications

This program will bring energy, passion and purpose back into a corporation. It provides a simple foundation of Success principles to motivate and engage employees. The company all the way down to the individuals Purpose will be defined. A new empowered corporate mindset will be employed and the 3 Finish lines to any goal will be presented in a fun, engaging and dynamic way. My messages speak to every person in the company regardless of position.

When you bring James into your business for a keynote speech, he makes himself open for the entire day with additional 'Break-out' Sessions to help your business promote a more healthy living in mind, body and spirit.

BREAK-OUT SESSION PROGRAMS

***Stumbling to Stepping Stones:* People without Purpose, Perish.**
Are you waking up in the morning stuck, unmotivated, feeling deep desire for something 'more' but don't know what? Purpose is what you are looking for. What are the 3 factors or a Purposeful Life? Leave this session with your own answer to the question, "What am I here for? What is my purpose in life?"

***F.O.C.U.S. and Motivation:* The Cycle of Success and Achievement**
Are you or your friends stuck in a rut? Have they lost their mojo and desire? Keeping yourself and others engaged in the Cycle of Success is critical. Learn how to stay happier, more satisfied and engaged in your work. The Motivational Football approach will keep you confident and empowered.

***Creating Conversation:* The Power of Language for Persuasion, Purpose and Profits**
One of the biggest reasons for letting a person go in business is poor communication. Powerful, purposeful communication is essential for managing, selling and effective leadership. Discover how to communicate more effectively consciously and unconsciously with others. Learn how to displace resistance to new ideas and find more ways of effectively creating change through speech.

***Accelerated Learning:* Producing the Highest Grades in the Best Time**
Have you ever felt there had to be an easier way to study? Do you suffer from test anxiety and undue stress. Unfortunately, we were never taught how to use our brain effectively to excel in school. Learn cutting edge tools, processes and exercises guaranteed to raise your grades at least one level in this incredible breakthrough session.

***Creating Conversation:* The Power of Language for Persuasion, Purpose and Profits**
One of the biggest reasons for letting a person go in business is poor communication. Powerful, purposeful communication is essential for managing, selling and effective leadership. Discover how to communicate more effectively consciously and unconsciously with others. Learn how to displace resistance to new ideas and find more ways of effectively creating change through speech.

<u>The Power of Money:</u> 3 Guiding Principles for Security, Safety and Responsible Living
Doe you get scared when the subject of money comes up? Are you afraid of managing what you have? Are you afraid of losing it all? Discover the 3 simple, fundamental steps to create all of the financial security, safety and abundance you desire. Money Mastery is Magical.

<u>From Madness to Meditation:</u> Stress Release for Health, Energy and a Vibrant Life
Are you stressed? Does tension wrack your mind, body and spirit? Meditation has been proven to boost energy, release tension and stress and increase health and wellness. Learn the two reasons to meditate, how to 'meditate on the light', and improve your life. It is easy, simple and anyone can do it. Stay calm and carry on.

Call now for more information on how you can bring James into your company for a powerful day of training!

(919) 792-0085 Office
(919) 745-7569 Cell
james@evolutionforsuccess.com

www.evolutionforsuccess.com
www.30DaysforSuccess.com
www.businessmarketingforsuccess.com